WRITING YOUR WAY TO RECOVERY

How Stories Can Save Our Lives

James Brown

and

Patrick O'Neil

Also by James Brown

Apology to the Young Addict
The Los Angeles Diaries
This River
Lucky Town
Final Performance
The Second Story Theatre & Two Encores

Also by Patrick O'Neil

Gun, Needle, Spoon

Praise for James Brown

"James Brown, already among the best memoirists in America, has surpassed his own high standards in *Apology to the Young Addict*. This superbly written book is about addiction, yes, but it is equally a book about courage, perseverance, love, desperation, recovery, and healing. More than anything, it is a book that reminds us, again and again, of the power of storytelling. In the pages of this heartbreaking but oddly exhilarating memoir, Brown deploys his narrative skills with precision, grace, complexity, and masterfully controlled intensity of emotion. What a fine piece of work."

Tim O'Brien, author of *The Things They Carried*

"The best addiction memoirs reflect on the running and gunning with just the right amount of thoughtful remove, which is exactly what makes James Brown's *The Los Angeles Diaries* so important…The book has more than enough material to justify a woe–is—me stance—an arsonist mother and suicidal siblings, to start with—but a clear–headed voice that mines the subject matter of regret while refusing to ever wallow keeps the narrator out of self-pity. Underread and underrated, Brown's vibrant imagery and nimble storytelling elevates *The Los Angeles Diaries* into a league all its own."

— *The Fix*, selected as one of the Ten Best Addiction Memoirs

"*This River* is a must read for any clinicians dealing with patients with substance abuse and dependency issues and also for patients and their families."

— Ana E. Campo, MD,
Addictive Disorders & Their Treatment

Praise for Patrick O'Neil

"Ever wondered what it would be like to live your wildest fantasy and your darkest nightmare at the same time? In this skillful turn, Patrick O'Neil's *Gun, Needle, Spoon* has saved you the trouble. A ferocious story of survival and redemption, only the beating, honest heart at the core of this sensational book will convince you that every word is true."

Jillian Lauren, *New York Times* bestselling author of *Some Girls: My Life in a Harem*

"Patrick O'Neil is the kind of literary character who doesn't usually live to tell his own story, who too often has to be rendered and re-imagined by a writer who played it safer from the sidelines. The fact that O'Neil—a haunted, hunted outlaw, as well an uproariously funny observer of society—is able to give voice to his own complex and dangerous story would be enough to distinguish *Gun, Needle, Spoon* from most other books. But O'Neil is also the real deal as a writer, full of frenetic energy, unsettling tenderness, and dialogue that sounds like he's smuggled a tape recorder to hell and back. A one of a kind read."

Gina Frangello, author of *A Life in Men*

Writing Your Way to Recovery: How Stories Can Save Our Lives

Copyright © 2021 by James Brown and Patrick O'Neil. All rights reserved.

No part of this publication may be reproduced, distributed, or transmitted in any form or by any means, including photocopying, recording, or other electronic or mechanical methods, without the prior written permission of the publishers, except in the case of brief quotations embodied in critical reviews and certain other noncommercial uses permitted by copyright law.

Author Website: www.jamesbrownauthor.com
Author Website: www.patrick-oneil.com

ISBN: 978-1-7368847-0-6

Requests to publish work from this book should be sent to:

Jbrown513a@yahoo.com

Cover Art: Andy Brown
Cover Design: Simpson & Bell
Author Photographer for James Brown: Nathan Brown
Author Photographer for Patrick O'Neil: Brian Looby

First Edition

To all the alcoholics and addicts out there, and there are millions of us, this book is dedicated to you and your recovery.

Forgive Us Our Sins, Or Something Along
Those Lines 51
Patrick O'Neil

Triggers 57
James Brown

Play the Tape All the Way Through 63
Patrick O'Neil

Close Calls and Narrow Escapes 69
James Brown

The "R" Word 77
Patrick O'Neil

It's Not Just About You (And It Never Was) ... 87
James Brown

How Can You Tell When a Junkie Is Lying? ... 95
Patrick O'Neil

Finding Your Inner Childish Asshole......... 101
James Brown

Writing Through the Wreckage of Our Past .. 111
Patrick O'Neil

Putting It All Together..................123
JAMES BROWN

So What Do We Do with This Book Now?...135
JAMES BROWN

So What Is This Book About?

James Brown

It's about looking at yourself. It's about looking *inside* yourself and better understanding who you are, what makes you tick, and why. I could be talking about anyone here, but I'm thinking about people like me and my co-author Patrick O'Neil. Alcoholics. Addicts.

We wanted to escape our feelings. We wanted to numb ourselves. We wanted to kill the thoughts rolling around in our heads, and if a drug or a drink did it for us, what was the harm? All we were after was a little escape from the drudgeries of life. And in the beginning, at least, getting loaded seemed to do the trick.

We enjoyed getting high.

We enjoyed getting drunk. But give it some time. If you're like Patrick and me, and tens of millions of others, you'll eventually find yourself alone and lost, cut off from your loved ones and the world as you once knew it.

The question is, how do we turn our lives around and get back on track? There's no easy answer, and certainly not one that applies to us all. A.A. works for many but not everyone and the same can be said of the different approaches and methodologies of the hundreds of rehabs across the country.

I wish Patrick and I had the solution, but if we pretended that we did, we'd be like all the other addiction gurus and self-help authors who tout ridiculously high success rates for saving people like us from self-destructing. This isn't to say that the so-called experts don't have our best interests at heart. I'm sure most do. But Patrick and I are cynics, as most alcoholic-addicts are, and I'm inclined to believe that some in the recovery community are simply out to make a buck off our misery.

The one thing we've noticed, however, the one thing the many programs and methods of recovery seem to have in common is the use of journaling.

Write about your addiction, they say.

Write about your feelings. Write about your thoughts. Write about your resentments, likes and dislikes, your fears and anger. Write about all the drugs you took and all the booze you drank and all the insane things you did while you were high or drunk. Other times they just want you to *vent*, as if venting alone will alleviate your rage, self-pity, self-loathing, anger, guilt and pain. And maybe sometimes it does. We're not saying journaling isn't useful. It is. The sheer act of writing is in and of itself a great way to confront our emotions and thoughts and their possible psychological connections to our addiction.

Journaling is one of many tools used in recovery, and it's a fine one, but could we do more with it? Could we do something different with writing that might be as helpful if not more so than journaling, or at the least a therapeutic adjunct to it?

Patrick and I think we can.

That's why we've written this book.

The idea, as I said in the beginning, is to look at yourself. But does that mean you necessarily have to write solely about yourself to better understand who you are, what makes you tick, and why? My friend and I don't believe it does.

Not exactly, anyway.

With distance comes clarity. And with clarity comes a greater sense of truth. That person on the page of your journal is and is not you. In our exercises you can make things up or draw from your own personal experience. Given the license to create, whether you fictionalize an event or person, or tell it like it really happened, you're bound to uncover truths about yourself and others that you'd never find through journaling alone.

Together, if you add it up, my friend and I spent roughly 50 years abusing dope and booze. For Patrick, 18 of those years were as a full-blown IV junkie. For me, in the beginning, the needle was an off-and-on occasion, but toward the end it became my preferred method of delivery. Faster acting. Bigger bang for the buck.

But Patrick and I now also share between us over three decades of sobriety.

I've spent about that same number of years teaching literature and creative writing as a Professor of English. I've written novels. I've written short stories and screenplays and three memoirs dealing with drug and alcohol addiction, suicide and madness. Patrick has also published a memoir, *Gun, Needle, Spoon*, covering his life in the world of punk rock, his slide into addiction and armed robbery. One more arrest and he would've been doing 25-to-life rather than writing this book with me. Today, with an M.F.A. under his belt, he, too, has taught creative writing at the university level as well as in prisons. And he's a Certified Drug and Alcohol Counselor currently working in the recovery community. In fact, he's done such exemplary work helping other alcoholic-addicts that he was given a Governor's Pardon by California Governor Jerry Brown in 2016.

Writing has helped us both to get clean and sober and stay that way. Now it's time to take what we've learned about writing and literature and apply it to the recovery process through techniques of storytelling designed to help people like us express ourselves, creatively, without the fear of being judged.

That judging goes for things like grammar, too.

Don't worry about spelling or where the commas and periods are supposed to go. This isn't high school. You're not being graded. A messy first draft is a good first draft. Just relax and write.

Patrick and I have assembled a series of writing exercises that deal with real-life issues facing those in recovery. One exercise, for instance, focuses on relapse and asks you to create an alcoholic-addict character coming home after leaving rehab. They've got six months clean and sober and want to keep it. But what sort of triggers and pitfalls are they likely to encounter returning to their neighborhood?

Another exercise deals with God and how the very notion of one sends a lot of us running out the doors of A.A. Do we really need to believe in a Higher Power to get clean and sober? For that matter, what does God or spirituality have to do with recovery anyway?

Other exercises are based on the Twelve Steps of Alcoholics Anonymous, such as forgiveness, honesty, and confronting the hurt we've caused others. Or Step One, where we must admit that "we were powerless over alcohol -- that our lives had become unmanageable." A lot of these exercises can be fun to do, but Patrick and I would be remiss if we didn't add that they could also be dangerous.

If you draw on material from your own past, some of the assignments may take you back to a time in your life that you'd prefer not to revisit, and if going there is too painful, too stressful, it could put you at risk of relapse. Alcoholic-addicts aren't the greatest when it comes to handling stress or pain. These feelings are, in part, what might've contributed to our drinking and using in the first place, and you may have to hit the brakes and stop writing if you find yourself getting too uncomfortable.

At the same time, a certain level of uncomfortableness is necessary and unavoidable in the recovery process. Self-examination doesn't generally bring back wonderful memories, and it's memories, like feelings of guilt and resentment, that we ultimately have to confront in getting clean and sober. The key here is striking the right balance as to what we can safely handle emotionally and what we can't.

And this balance is elusive.

What you're capable of handling today may not be the same tomorrow. Or vice-versa. Sometimes we have to take two steps back to help us leap forward. Recovery doesn't necessarily follow a linear path, or at least it didn't for Patrick and me. We can't and shouldn't speak as if we're some sort of ultimate authorities on recovery.

We're not.

As alcoholic-addicts we have only our experience, strength and hope to offer. And as authors and teachers, we add to this offer the small but perhaps very important tool of creative writing.

Getting Started

Patrick O'Neil

I'm not someone that grew up excited about writing and knowing they were going to be a writer. In fact when I was young I suffered from dyslexia and had trouble in school. My learning disability was undiagnosed until I was an adult. Hey, it was a long time ago, the educational system didn't really care about that kind of "psychological stuff" back in the '60's.

All my life I've verbally transposed numbers, which translates to do-not-ask-me for a phone number, and math has always been a mystery. But the worst is, I have difficulty pronouncing words, mainly names, and even today there are some that just do not look as if they're spelled correctly, even though I know they are (thank the universe for computers and spell check).

I guess in response, or maybe frustration, I turned to telling stories visually as an artist. By the age of 14 I was the youngest nationally published cartoonist in America. At 17 I got a free ride to the San Francisco Art Institute and majored in film. While I was studying in school two things happened, punk rock and heroin. Somewhere in there I stopped creating art and started playing music.

Segue to 20 years later and I was facing a three strikes case of 25-to-life for armed robbery, more specifically bank robbery, and I'll let you in on a little not-so-secret, it wasn't the punk rock that got me there.

If you've attended an A.A. meeting you no doubt have heard more than a few folks proudly proclaim that "getting arrested saved my life," and probably thought, *yeah okay, sure if you say so.* But in my case it really did. As a dope fiend I was not on the fast track for success. It was more a slow dance with death, or incarceration for life on the installment plan.

On my 41st birthday I was on the yard at San Quentin wondering how my life had gone so far astray. Why had I stopped caring about creating art, music, and appreciating the beauty of all the things that mattered to my 17-year-old artist self?

Took me a few attempts but I was eventually able to re-embrace creativity and find my self-expression with writing. I started when I was locked up in county jail, then I joined a writer's group in prison, and I kept at it when I was released on parole.

I found my inspiration in the world around me. I wrote short nonfiction bits about the people I knew, crimes I committed, or exploratory essays about what my life had been like as compared to what it was now.

To stay off drugs I joined A.A. and N.A. and found sobriety. As service to others I began working in treatment as a drug and alcohol counselor. I wanted to give back this gift of sobriety that had been given so freely to me.

At six years sober I returned to school for an MFA in Creative Writing with an emphasis in nonfiction prose. I wrote as my thesis what would eventually become my memoir, *Gun, Needle, Spoon*. A year after graduation I was assistant teaching freshman English at a community college. Another three years and *Gun, Needle, Spoon* was published in France. A few years later it came out in America.

I've since taught college-level writing courses, lectured at universities, and facilitated workshops. And I've published nearly two hundred fiction and non-fiction works for numerous journals, anthologies, websites, and literary magazines.

Yet when Jim reached out with a proposal to collaborate on this project I immediately went to a place of fear. Was I a good enough writer? Would Jim see through this façade I project to fool everyone else? Would I let him down? Because deep down inside I still feel like that fearful drug addict screw-up whose life was a mess, that same dyslexic kid ashamed that he couldn't read or write.

I guess what I'm trying to say here is that no matter how far I've come there will always be that negative voice that started well before drugs and alcohol sounded like the answer to all my problems. Even with 20 years of sobriety I am still prone to self-doubt. I have a big ego and low self-esteem. If I let them, my fears will rule me.

I tell my wife these disparaging thoughts and fears and she says, "That's because you have alcoholism."

Of course she's right.

I know this may sound repetitive, grandiose, and overly exaggerated, but similar to getting arrested, writing saved my life.

Yes, it literally did.

I'm someone that needs a passion in order to exist. Before it was art, then music, then heroin, and now it's the written word. Writing has also given me a purpose and an identity, but even more than that a much-needed outlet to confront my demons.

I hope that what Jim and I present in this book can help you, too. There is power in the written word. Power to heal and explore. As Jim has already mentioned, journaling is a crucial component to recovery. And let's not forget the writing involved with Step work. Yet opening that blank page to write can still feel daunting.

Plus with our writing exercises we're just giving you the premise. It's on you to begin the work. There's no one hovering over your shoulder urging you on. For a lot of writers that's difficult territory, especially when being asked to examine our past and really look inside ourselves.

So if starting to write is something you're having trouble with, then for just a quick minute put all that apprehension and fear aside, and let's start with a simple exercise that could help jump-start this whole thing.

***

Pick four consecutive days this week and set aside 20 minutes each day where you can write without interruption (if you can't put together four consecutive days, then just do the exercise on the four days that you can). For the first five minutes think or meditate on your mental outlook, emotions, alcoholism, using, drinking, addiction, past trauma; and how they've affected you, your life, your relationships, your past, your present, and your future.

Think of how it has affected who you have been, who you would like to be, and who you are now. Think of your addiction from your perspective, another involved person's perspective (if there was one), or a non-involved person's perspective. Push past all those mental cobwebs, access your rawest emotions, and put a name to them. Identify any guilt, fear, shame, resentments, ego, and anger that you had, or are still experiencing.

Now set a timer for 10 minutes. During this time you will be writing nonstop stream of consciousness. Once you put the pen to paper or your fingers to the keyboard continue until the time is up. Do not stop to think about what you are writing (that was what the first five minutes of meditation were for).

Instead, free write your memories, thoughts, and feelings. Do not worry about spelling, grammar, or sentence structure. You won't be sharing this with anyone. This is just for you. Your page count is whatever you produce. So let go of any fears of not meeting that requirement.

After you're done give yourself five minutes where you can relax and let go of everything you've just written about.

* * *

One of the most satisfying results of this exercise is seeing the pages of writing you produce. Maybe none of it is coherent enough to immediately get published, but I'm willing to bet there are ideas and sections that can later be incorporated into a first draft.

Hopefully the proposed time structure and daily commitment will open the door for you to start your writing practice. I know for me the "You won't be sharing this with anyone" clause was a great relief. Sometimes we just need a nudge to get us going.

It is also an excellent tool for working out a scene or story where we're not quite sure of what it's about or where we want to take it. By using this free-flowing train of thought process we can tap into our unconscious emotions, allowing us to discover things that have not been so obvious.

However I do want to pass on a very valuable lesson I've learned over the years. My writing practice consists of sitting down everyday to write. Some days I knock out a few thousand words and it's amazing and everything I love about writing. Then there are days I barely hunt-and-peck 50 words, and it can be depressing. Yet what I have learned is that no matter what I write that day, 50 or a thousand words, the book still gets written.

I used to berate myself for those low word count days. Now I'm good with whatever I write that day.

Maybe this recovery stuff is working?

The Beginning of the End

James Brown

I don't know how many times I swore that this was the end. No more drinking. No more using. I was finished. Done. Invariably I made this vow the morning after an especially crazy night, or a string of crazy nights and days combined, when I was hungover and sick to my stomach. And sick of myself for whatever stupid and dangerous things I'd done while I was wasted, assuming I could remember any of it.

I hated being dependent on alcohol and drugs.

I hated the man I'd become, assuming, again, that I could even remember who that person was. The longer I drank and used, the harder it became to muster up those better memories of my former self. Because I started so early in life, with my first hit of marijuana at age nine and my first drink at 12, I had to draw on the brief periods of my life when I wasn't under the influence of something or another. That didn't leave me much to work with, as I was drinking daily by my twenties while using, although not regularly yet, just about everything else I could get my hands on.

For some of us, Patrick included, drugs and alcohol became a way of life before our lives had hardly begun. What's weird, though, is that even if you classify me as an alcoholic-addict at an early age, I still always felt, deep down, in my heart, that there was a better person inside of me. And that person, that unrealized part of me, was capable of saving and transforming my out-of-control life. I just had to find him.

Except finding him wasn't easy.

I made my first real attempt to get sober when I was 40. I'm coming up on 15 years of sobriety now, but I'm 63-years-old as I write this, so that means it took me about 23 years to get that precious 15. What happened to those other eight years? Or should I say, what happened *during* those other eight years that prevented me from cleaning up? The answer is simple. Me. I was the problem. I was my own worst enemy.

I'd go to A.A., listen to what then seemed to me like a lot of bullshit, maybe white-knuckle it for a few days, then go back out. I'd drink and use again for a few months, get my ass kicked, and then, with my tail between my legs, slink back into the rooms of A.A. Maybe this time I'd stay sober for a month or two -- enough, anyway, to start feeling healthy. It'd been so long since I'd felt healthy that I'd forgotten what it was like *not* to wake up hung-over, *not* to look in the mirror at my bloodshot eyes and bloated face. Feeling and seeing the difference was a strange but amazing experience for me, and I liked it. I liked it a lot.

But was it enough to keep me sober?

Of course not. What's health when out of the blue you find yourself obsessing over that first drink or drug and you don't have sense enough to think about how it always takes you straight back to the bottom again.

In a later exercise by Patrick, he writes about "playing the tape through," which is about how we fixate on how good the drugs and alcohol made us feel rather than remembering where they ultimately led us. That's me, time and again, forgetting about the darkness and despair of addiction and caving into the obsession to drink and use.

Some say that you have to hit bottom before you can turn your life around, but I'm not so sure that's true. I've hit bottom multiple times. And multiple times I've gotten sober only to mess up again.

If you're a chronic relapser, you understand where I'm coming from. If you're not, if you got clean and sober the first time you decided you'd had enough, that's great. I admire you. I envy you. But we all need to keep this in mind: if there's one thing we don't want to do, it's judge one another. We each get sober in our own time, and I've seen many so-called hopeless cases eventually prove the doubters dead wrong.

As I said earlier, I don't know how many times I swore off drinking and using and then blew it. But I do recall my last bottom, the one preceding my current and longest stint of continuous sobriety, and it was with a dear friend in Sacramento, California. My marriage had fallen apart, I'd fallen apart, and I wanted to spend some time with my friend.

Talk things out.

Think things through. My friend's health was also failing and I knew he might not be long for the world. We needed to see each other. We needed to spend some time together.

The drive to his place was about five-hundred miles, and when I got there my nerves were shot. I craved a drink. He had a bottle waiting for me, that and much more. Doctors had prescribed him all sorts of medications to ease his pain, from Percocet to injectable morphine sulfate, and my friend was generous. He was also, as they say in recovery, "one of us," though oddly I never thought of him as an alcoholic-addict. We'd just always partied hard together, going all the way back to when we first became friends as teenagers.

For three days straight we drank, popped painkillers, and shot-up morphine sulphate. The first day was good, and by good I mean we got good and wasted. All my worries, troubles and concerns faded into oblivion. That second and third day, however, it seemed that no matter how much I drank, how many pills I popped, or how much dope I put in my arm, I couldn't for the life of me get out of my head. And I was obviously borderline od'ing. Maybe my body was relaxed, but my mind wouldn't shut down. I couldn't escape my feelings and thoughts. I barely felt high. I wasn't getting anywhere near the relief I wanted.

In A.A., I've heard members of the fellowship say that at the end of their drinking and using days the "drugs and alcohol just stopped working." But I never took it literally. Even now, I doubt they mean it literally. But that was exactly the case for me. It sounds physiologically impossible to continue to consume large amounts of drugs and alcohol without shutting down the consciousness, but I'm not making this up. I'm not lying. I'll admit that my body eventually rejected the poisons I put into it, and I spent some memorable time in the bathroom, my head in the toilet. Short of that, the booze and drugs simply weren't doing their job, and when I left for home the fourth day, I was physically ill for a solid week. Just thinking about drinking or putting more drugs into my body made me nauseous, and I fell into a deep depression.

That was the last time I got drunk and high, when the booze and dope quit doing what they were supposed to do, and it scared the hell out of me.

If I couldn't kill my feelings and thoughts with alcohol and drugs, the only other viable alternative was to permanently shut down the brain myself. Or so I figured. I did have one other choice. For me, in the end, sobriety really was a matter of life or death.

So what does this guy who couldn't escape himself want you to do with the story he just shared?

THE BEGINNING OF THE END

What would his co-author suggest? I have a feeling Patrick and I are on the same page here. Someone who was once looking at 25-to-life must've considered his full array of options as they compared to getting sober or dying behind bars.

How about this?

Tell us about the beginning of the end of your drinking and using days.

* * *

In two-to-three pages, write about the last time you promised yourself that you'd never drink or use again. That you were done. Finished. Hopefully the first time was the last time you made this vow, but regardless, I want you to relive it. I want you to write it as a scene.

Where were you when you made the decision?

How did you arrive at it? Why? Did something terrible happen to make you swear off? Was it an accumulation of things? Were others involved?

Did you think about your loved ones?

Did you want to clean up for them as much as for yourself?

Or did you just wake up one morning, look in the mirror and decide enough was enough?

How about an arrest? A DUI? Was there any one event, person, place or thing that made you say to yourself that you had to change, no more excuses, no ifs or buts about it. Be completely honest. There's no right or wrong way to do this assignment. Just tell the truth about how you felt and thought when you made for the first or umpteenth time the decision to get sober.

* * *

When you're done, set it aside. Take a deep breath. Relax for 10 or 15 minutes. Then, as Patrick suggests in one of his later exercises, talk to "someone in recovery, or at least someone who understands addiction." Writing intense, personal stuff can help us with our recovery as well as put it in jeopardy, so do some self-maintenance. And please don't forget, not for a second, that in making record of the end of our drinking and using days, you're affirming the beginning of a new life free of the bondage of addiction.

Who the Hell Am I?

Patrick O'Neil

Acceptance is another word that gets tossed around a lot in recovery. But what does it really mean? Traditionally acceptance has been defined as receiving what is being offered, and the act of believing. Which sounds a lot like recovery or maybe just one of those not so thinly veiled proverbs from the Bible.

When I think back to early sobriety I wasn't really receptive or inclined to trust what I was being told. My life was chaotic; an endless parade of difficult situations, one after another, bombarding me and getting under my skin. I was angry, but I didn't really know why, or at what. I was resentful at everybody and everything. I didn't understand that I was the problem. It was me that had to change. Not everyone else.

From day one I was told I needed to find acceptance or I wasn't going to stay sober. Yet my initial reaction was, "I don't know if I'm capable of doing this." My thoughts were filled with all the "could have, would have, should haves." I didn't get the god thing. I didn't feel a part of anything. I was uncomfortable in my own skin.

I'd be at a meeting complaining how hard it all was and then some old-timer would ramble off The Serenity Prayer:

God, grant me the serenity to accept the things I cannot change, the courage to change the things I can, and the wisdom to know the difference.

Which just made me even more self-conscious and I would stop talking, roll my eyes, and keep my thoughts to myself. I didn't think anyone with long-term sobriety could possibly understand what I was going through. I couldn't accept that praying would somehow "fix" everything or even change how I felt.

To be honest, in the beginning The Serenity Prayer totally pissed me off. It was just one more riddle to decipher in the long line of riddles that made up recovery. As if staying clean wasn't hard enough. Plus what the hell was this god stuff about. I wasn't religious.

To say I was the antithesis of acceptance would not have been an understatement. I was the poster boy for un-acceptance: difficult, combative, argumentative, and unwilling. Even though I knew that drugs and alcohol had kicked my ass, I had a hard time accepting that the past was over, that this was where and who I was, and that my future was now about staying sober or dying.

I would sit in the back of the meeting glaring at everyone, wondering why, if the newcomer was so important, that no one was talking to me. It's a classic example of pulling someone into a hug while at the same time pushing them away. You can't have it both ways.

Being an addict had been my whole identity. So who the hell was I now? I can remember a TV commercial back in the '80's where kids were asked what they wanted to be when they grew up and they answered, "a fireman," or "a ballerina," or "a track-star." While the overdubbed narrator smugly proclaimed, "Nobody says they want to be a junkie when they grow up." I was in my 20's and using heavily on a daily basis. I not only wanted to be a junkie. I was a junkie.

By the time I sought sobriety my addiction and alcoholism were so ingrained into who I thought I was that it was really difficult to visualize myself as someone that didn't drink and use. Yet on the flip side I look back at who I was before I got sober and I don't even recognize that person either. With this conflicting shift in identity it's not surprising that I had no real sense of who I was.

Which brings us to the next writing exercise.

* * *

For this one we're going to write three or more pages about ourselves in the third person (he/she/they, not the first person of I/me). To write this you're going to assume the role of someone else, as if you actually were that person, and think about how they would describe you: physically, your attitude, your emotional state, your physical surroundings, and any other details that define you. This is to be solely from an outsider's perspective. Not who or what we hope others see us as.

If you need visual help, start by taking a long hard look in the mirror. I know. Not always my favorite pastime either.... "Where did all those extra pounds around my waist come from?"

Another source could be photos or even videos you might have lying around. With the latter you can really see your mannerisms, which are great details.

This exercise can be difficult as you might naturally slip into describing the person that you want to be seen and known as. That doesn't mean you are not to include all your good attributes. Just be careful to straddle the line on what we want to project and who we really are.

At the same time avoid all the self-depreciating mental put-downs, overly critical judgments, or the need to make excuses for our behaviors. In other words, be impartial, fair, and… here we go, write from a place of acceptance.

As I said, set the goal for at least three pages. Go deep with this. Pull the covers off and let you (and the world) see you.

When you've finished invite somebody you trust, and whose opinion you care about, to read it. Ask them if this represents how they see you. If there are discrepancies, or they say that there are things you've left out, make notes, and then revise.

Put it away for a day. Reread it. Has your perspective changed? Do you need to add anything that is different today?

***

As Jim and I can readily attest, in recovery we are a work in progress. The final product of this exercise will probably evolve over time if you revisit it again. Naturally we age. But there are other less obvious changes. I know my expression has softened over the past twenty years. I no longer have to project an aura of hostility. I even smile now and then.

Please, Not Step One Again

James Brown

Okay, so you recognize that you can't safely drink or use anymore. You probably wouldn't be reading this now if you could. I'm sure you have better things to do with your time than listen to an alcoholic-addict who's been indoctrinated by A.A. tell you time and again that you have to admit to being a drunk or junkie before you can do anything about it. It makes sense. You get it, damn it. But what about the second part of Step One where you're supposed to concede that your life "had become unmanageable." Really?

Who wants to admit defeat? Not me.

I'm a stubborn bastard. Listening to some of the stories in A.A., I used to compare myself to others who had lost more than me and think, hey, I'm not *that* far gone. Maybe these other people are total losers, but not me, and I took pleasure in thinking that I was somehow better than them because I hadn't sunk as far. After all I still had my house. I still had my job. So my wife and I weren't getting along (to put it mildly), but what marriages don't have a few problems? Did that mean my life was out of control?

No way.

I just had a problem with drinking and maybe an occasional issue with the recreational use of methamphetamine, coke and heroin. I love that word *recreational* as it applies to narcotics, as if sticking a needle in your arm or putting meth up your nose is just another family-fun way to spend your leisure time, like going to Disneyland or playing Frisbee.

Truth is, my life *was* unmanageable.

I couldn't get through a day without drinking. And once I was drunk, I'd started looking for other drugs, and I knew where to find them. Invariably, without going into the sordid details, this led to a world of pain and trouble and insane behavior. But, like I said, I'm a stubborn bastard, I wasn't going down without a fight, and so I had a constant battle with two voices in my head.

One told me that maybe I had a problem, sure, but by no means was life unmanageable. Things weren't nearly as bad as I made them out to be and I could turn it around if I only tried harder. It was a simple matter of will power. Mind over matter.

Yeah, right.

The other voice told me that I'd made a mess of my life and the sooner I admitted it, the sooner I could get to work trying to put it back together. My world had spiraled out of control long ago, only I couldn't see it. Or I refused to see it. And quitting drinking and using, I've come to learn, is not a simple matter of will power.

I needed help and I needed it badly.

It was as if I had a devil sitting on one side of my shoulder whispering lies into my ear and an angel on the other telling me the hard truths I didn't want to hear. I doubt I'm alone with this experience.

* * *

So what I want you to do, in two-to-three pages, is write a dialogue replicating the two voices in your head, one telling you that your life is a mess, the other telling you the opposite. Or, if you're still wrestling with admitting that you're "powerless over alcohol," have one voice argue that you're not a real alcoholic and the other that you are. It could go something like this:

"I don't have a problem with drinking."

"Like hell you don't."

"I can quit any time I want."

"Then why do you drink everyday?"

"Because it helps take the edge off."

"Off what?"

"The day. I have a stressful job."

"What job? You lost it."

"That wasn't because of my drinking."

"Of course not. But calling in sick every Monday for the last two months because you were hung over probably didn't help. Losing your temper and screaming at your co-workers isn't a great idea, either. Look at your hands. They're shaking. Bet a nice big shot of vodka would take care of that."

And on it goes.

You're basically putting into words the argument that you've undoubtedly played over and over in your head before you finally came to accept that you're a bona fide alcoholic-addict and your life was seriously in need of repair.

Ideally, assuming you're the real deal and have come to realize it, I'd like you to end the dialogue with the voice that tells you the truth about yourself. The voice arguing differently needs to lose the debate. Most importantly, the prevailing voice shouldn't end on a note of condemnation, regret or shame, but rather one of hope, promise, and the courage to change.

"If I can get sober," it might say, "anyone can. You're not alone."

Oh No, Is He Talking About God Again?

Patrick O'Neil

My sponsor hates it when I talk about feeling like an agnostic, or an atheist, or just conflicted and confused. He definitely believes in God, capital "G" and all. But you know I'm not so sure about god. In truth I had, and sometimes still do have, a lot of trouble with the concept of a higher power.

Now if you don't, then all the more power to you. And maybe this chapter isn't for you, or maybe it is? But for a lot of us the god part of A.A. was a roadblock we had to navigate around if we wanted to remain in the fellowship and stay sober.

Unfortunately quite a few of us had religion shoved down our throats as children, typically of the sort that damned you for being who you were. Then we showed up at our first meeting, and boom, it's god all over again. Not so oddly the statistics say A.A. loses a large percentage of newcomers due to its thinly veiled Christianity.

I grew up in a very conflicted household, especially when it came to religion. My mother was a quasi-Catholic-sometime-Protestant that would force us kids to go to church on a not so regular basis. My father was a Marxist. On Sunday, he'd say, "you can go to church if you want, but I'm going out to hike in the woods and then eat doughnuts and drink hot chocolate. You want to go, too?" My mother's response was something along the lines that we were all going to hell (and after my dad finally left for good, she definitely prayed that's where he was).

I'm laying odds you could easily guess what a six-year-old wanted to do more than go to Sunday school. So every time I read "God" in the Big Book I'd think of my dad. Which brought up all those old conflicting feelings of wanting to please an authority figure as opposed to rebelling.

Back then I had a sponsor I would later learn was what they called a "Big Book Thumper," and he didn't really care or understand my issues with religion and god. Anytime I expressed doubt and a lack of faith he would tell me to read, "We the Agnostics" because he said, "A.A. is a spiritual, not a religious program." But then two seconds later he was telling me I had to pray.

As a newcomer it seemed impossible to separate religion and spirituality. When asked if there was a power greater than myself I'd mumble "the universe." But really what I was thinking was the California Department of Corrections' ability to lock me up and take away my freedom. Now that was an undeniable power greater than me. But I sure as hell wasn't turning my will and my life over to the "care" of the CDC again. If I truly did have a higher power it would never lock me in a cell for 23 hours a day with a serial killer (true story).

So what does all this talk of a higher power and spirituality have to do with writing your way to recovery? Well if you read a lot of addiction memoirs, or just memoirs in general, you'll notice there's a connecting tissue that most of them have. Memoir often embraces seemingly un-embraceable subjects such as death, loss, illnesses, catastrophes, squandered opportunities, horrific events, addiction, broken dreams, and then chronicle the protagonist's ability to overcome adversity and persevere.

But the memoirs that really resonate are when the authors reflect on their "journey" and use their story as an opportunity to look inside themselves. It's not just everything that they have experienced, but how everything has helped change them into who they are today — the person that is writing the memoir. That "internal change" is by definition spirituality, "the quality of being concerned with the human spirit or soul."

Whew, that took a long way to get here, right? Okay so again, you may be wondering, *what the hell is he talking about now?* And if I haven't lost you yet, here it is. Spirituality is not just what we need in a memoir; it's also what we need for our program of recovery.

I don't know about you, but I can be judgmental, opinionated, and self-centered at the drop of a hat. The littlest thing someone says can hurtle me off the cliff of self-righteousness.

Hell, if I'm being totally honest here, I can do all that by myself without anyone's help.

Plus there's a constant chatter going on in my brain, most of it not very admirable or kind. My first thought is not always my best thought. So usually I just keep it to myself, process it, and wait for a rebuttal, some compassion; or at the very least a spark of humanity that allows me to hold my head up and not wallow in a deep pool of self-obsession.

Yet even as I write that last paragraph I immediately think, *where the hell is my spirituality?* And then of course my second thought, *these people must think I'm a horrible human being.* See? I told you there was a lot of chatter.

So for me the concept of spirituality was a bit too ambiguous. Okay, so it's not god. It's not religion. It's... oh shit, I don't know what the hell it is.

A totally confusing quote that gets thrown around a lot at A.A. meetings is from the French priest and philosopher Pierre Teilhard de Chardin, who said, "We are not human beings having a spiritual experience. We are spiritual beings having a human experience."

Um… thanks. That really cleared it up for me.

Okay, not really.

Then one sunny afternoon I was driving on the freeway in Los Angeles and I passed a broken down and very overloaded station wagon on the side of the road. The hood was up, gray smoke billowing out, and a family huddled together on the shoulder. For a nanosecond I locked eyes with the mother as she hugged her child and I swear I could feel her sadness and absolute despair.

I was hemmed in between two lanes of speeding traffic and I really couldn't stop. Besides I didn't even know what help I could have been. I had no tools to help fix the car or spare money to pay for a tow off the freeway. Yet the fear in that woman's eyes haunted me and I remember thinking, *let those people be all right. Let that woman get her kids home safely.*

Now that might not seem like a big deal to you, and I understand. But for someone that used to drive by similar situations and think, *better you than me, sucker,* it was a huge departure. And in that moment I came that much closer to understanding spirituality. It wasn't that I had to attain nirvana, or make some magnanimous gesture, or even perform a miracle. I just had to give a shit about someone other than myself.

Of course your definition of spirituality may be different than mine, and I totally get that. In no way do I want to repeat the same mistake of how religion was forced onto me. These are just my thoughts, concepts and experiences. Yet what I am going to ask you to write about in this next exercise should be universally accepted. So here we go.

* * *

The assignment, in two-to-three pages (or more if you need it), is to write about an act of kindness that you've witnessed, experienced, engaged in, or yes, even made up. What I want to do here is to take a little departure from all the "heavy" material we'll be processing and write about a moment of beauty from our lives. Something that touched your soul. Where another person was cared for. A moment that restored your faith in humanity. That time you were selfless and supportive. Dig deep into that caring heart of yours.

But most of all find the emotions that were at play. Describe what you were feeling and let the reader know how it made you feel —- and maybe even how it still makes you feel.

* * *

Ultimately have some fun with this assignment. Not everything in recovery has to be so serious. This is a subject where I encourage you to get creative. Allow yourself to really see and feel that moment.

And always remember, with all writing, everything, and I do mean *everything*, is not only allowed to be revised, but encouraged. Maybe treat this as a first draft? Let it sit, come back to it, and revise accordingly.

As you may have noticed, I'm a big advocate of letting work sit and then returning to it. Fresh eyes allow for fresh ideas. Truth is my definition of spirituality has been evolving for years. Every time I think I've nailed it, a new sense of purpose arises and I'm back to revising what I thought was a final draft. But then I guess that's the beauty of spirituality. It ebbs and flows and becomes what it needs to be at the exact moment you need it.

God? Not God?

James Brown

Like Patrick, I had trouble with God. Since the ripe old age of seven, when my mother was arrested and thrown in jail, I sat on the lawn outside our apartment complex, looked up at the sky, and cursed Him. Or Her. Or It. I think I actually said "fuck you," fully expecting to be struck dead by lightening. It didn't happen. And in the mind of a child this was only further proof that He didn't exist. And if He did, as my older sister firmly believed and tried her best to make me believe, then what sort of God was He to allow our mother to be taken from us?

So began my life as an atheist, or, at best, an agnostic.

Believing or not believing in God didn't seem to present any problems for me until my forties. I got by just fine on my own, or so I thought, because by then I was a total mess. Nevertheless, when I first walked into the rooms of Alcoholics Anonymous, the "God thing" almost sent me running. By now I'd come to accept that I was "powerless over alcohol," and when push came to shove, though I resisted it for as long as I could, I also eventually had to admit that my life had "become unmanageable." Of course this is the First Step in A.A. and there's no point in attempting the next if you honestly don't think that you've fucked up just about everything in your life because you couldn't stop drinking and drugging.

But that Second Step?

It says that we have to believe in a "Power greater than ourselves," and it capitalizes the *P* in *power*, which is a dead giveaway that it's referring to God, thereby assuming that God exists. And that, as I said earlier, was a problem for me. Actually it's a problem for a lot of people, and I'm not just talking about A.A.

Patrick wrestles with this same issue, empathizing with those who had "religion shoved down [their] throats as children," predisposing them to later reject god. Especially the one spelled with a capital *G*. Even today, with 20 years of sobriety, his definition of spirituality continues to evolve.

I understand that. I respect that.

In time, however, I changed, but this doesn't mean that I don't or can't still identify with those who either downright don't believe in a God or are struggling to embrace one. For me the change occurred slowly, over a period of a couple years, when my sponsor kept after me to pray, to whom or what didn't matter, just pray, even if I only saw it as a one-sided conversation with myself.

"Open your mind to the *possibility* of a God," he said. "That's all I'm asking. And when you pray, keep it simple. At night, if you got through the day sober, hit your knees and say 'thank you.' And in the morning, when you wake up, hit your knees and ask for 'the strength' to do it again. What's that take out of your day? Thirty seconds? A minute? Don't tell me you can't do that."

Allowing for the possibility of a God involves an openness toward faith, and as the sober days began to accumulate, the simple act of prayer combined with a little faith eventually turned into a belief in God. Once that happened, the conversation was no longer one-sided. Obviously it's more complicated than this, requiring much soul-searching and willingness, confronting looming questions and doubt, but it's how the process began for me.

But that's just me.

What about you?

Is there a God, and, if so, who is He or She or It?

* * *

In two-to-three pages, describe the God of your own understanding. Do you picture Him as Christians picture Jesus? Is He or She or It different than the God of traditional world religions? Do you see this Power in terms of Mother Nature? The Great Spirit? The Collective Consciousness of Humankind? Does It defy personification? What strengths, virtues and qualities does your God possess? Kindness? Love? Is He forgiving or punishing or both?

For the non-believers, for the sake of argument, if you were to have a God, what would you like Him or Her or It to be? Again, you don't have to believe in a God, but you do have to pretend that if by some chance there was one, what might He or She or It mean to you? What would be Its strengths, virtues and qualities?

What we're after with this exercise is nothing more than a better grasp of a God of our own understanding. And we do it by articulating and describing who and what He or She or It means to each of us.

***

It's also my hope that we might stumble across some similarities between the believer and non-believer's hopes and beliefs. Can the non-believer get sober without God?

Sure.

I've seen it many times. But does a belief in God help in the recovery process? Speaking for myself, absolutely. It's made a huge difference for me and millions of others in and out of A.A. What I can say, unequivocally, is that believers and non-believers can and do get clean and sober together.

As Patrick so eloquently put it, "spirituality... ebbs and flows and becomes what it needs to be at the exact moment you need it."

Forgive Us Our Sins
Or Something Along Those Lines

PATRICK O'NEIL

If you drank and used for a few decades like Jim and I did, then you probably have a long list of people you have wronged. All those folks you lied to, cheated, ripped off, abandoned, ignored, manipulated, or just plain treated like shit. Because, you know, the booze and drugs were always way more important than anything else. Being a self-centered, self-absorbed, self-god-damn-everything is after all the nature of the addiction beast.

When I was strung-out my total focus was on one thing —getting, using, and wanting more. And woe is you if you got in my way. I lied to people when I could have told the truth. I took money under false pretenses. I used intimidation, force, and violence to support my habit. I was never there for anyone who needed me. I left a lot of hurt people in my wake.

Like a good majority of "career" addicts and alcoholics I started young. I began drinking and smoking when I was just a kid, right around 12 years old. The next few years I got into psychedelics and prescription pills. As an adolescent I discovered narcotics. By adulthood I was a full-blown junkie. At 43 I got sober. As one can well imagine being in the trenches for that long I created a whirlwind of chaos, drama, and destruction. And because of that I carry a lot of guilt and shame.

When I was using I was able to block-out all those uncomfortable feelings that dared to penetrate my opiated haze. But without alcohol and drugs all my pain, fear, and self-doubt are now forefront and center.

I actually hug them like long lost friends.

But if I don't do something about those feelings, take care of them, or at least come to terms with my part in the repercussive fallout from my past, then that shame and guilt become the new monkey on my back.

I hope this doesn't sound familiar, or worse it's something that you too have experienced. But my seemingly "favorite" pastime is to lie in bed at night staring at the ceiling as scene after scene of the worst moments of my life play in vivid Technicolor and Dolby sound on the letterbox wide-screen of my brain. Some are so real I swear I can smell fear in the air. Most are just jolts of electrified repulsion. Others are simply more abject proof of why I hold myself in such disregard.

I've become accustomed to calling this the "greatest hits" of my transgressions. They almost always start off something like this: I'm shaking. I'm dope sick and sweating. There's a metallic taste in my mouth and bile is building up in the back of my throat. I'm pointing a gun at a bank teller. Her eyes wide open in terror. A scream frozen silent on her lips.

This woman is someone's mom, sister, wife, or daughter. But at that very moment I don't care. All I want is money. Money to buy the heroin I so desperately need.

In my narcotic craving mind I can't comprehend the damage I'm doing. But now, many years later, I know. That woman will probably carry this moment with her for the rest of her life. Who wouldn't? A drug-crazed maniac waving a semi-automatic is threatening you for money that isn't even yours. Is the job even worth it? Did she go home to never return?

Of all the concepts of recovery, forgiveness is perhaps the most complex and challenging. In the beginning I didn't really get the whys, whats, and how-comes of forgiveness. I just wasn't capable of that kind of introspection. I was still stuck in that "I'm the victim" mentality. I blamed the cops for my incarceration. I blamed my parents, childhood, and the perceived bad hand I'd been dealt in life as an excuse for why I used the way I did. I was angry at the world for not seeing how brilliant I was, while barely producing anything that would garner attention, let alone recognition or fame.

When I heard people talk about forgiveness it felt like they were saying, "Okay sure, let's just give everyone else in the entire planet a break," and in my mind it was one they had never given me. Yet I was continually plagued by the memories of every violent, dishonest, and shameful thing I had ever done.

I don't remember where I heard it first, whether it was at a meeting, or a sponsor said it, or if I'd read it somewhere. But I can paraphrase it like this. You don't forgive them for them. You forgive *them* for *you*. Because you don't want to feel that pain every time you remember what they did.

Which is a beautiful and courageous sentiment. Yet how do you go about achieving this? Wave a magic wand? Think happy thoughts and snap your fingers?

Then I thought about the bank teller. Thought about her as a person. Not an extension of a financial institution. What her experience must have been like. How the results of my actions had affected her and those around her.

And then bam, I had one of those epiphany moments where things fell together and made sense. I could only be forgiven if I absolutely knew what I was asking forgiveness for. I had to understand and share the other person's feelings. As a writer this is not a hard concept to grasp. We do it all the time when we write characters. We embody that "person" and make them real so that the reader is invested in them enough to keep on reading.

* * *

So the exercise here, in two-to-three pages, is to be that person that you want to forgive you, and what this entails is writing from their perspective. Be the person you have wronged. Put yourself in their shoes and tell us why you are so resentful. Don't leave out any details. Give us the dirt, the hate, the anger, and the hurt. Don't be objective. Don't hold anything back. Don't be neutral. You want to find forgiveness? Let them tell you how.

Try to shoot for two-to-three pages, but give it more if possible, as you really want to get into this exercise. It's going to be the specific details that bring about the understanding of what the other person experienced and may even still be holding on to.

If using a real life scenario is too difficult, then write from a fictional place and detach yourself from the actual person and just write what happened from a fictional character's perspective. In the vernacular of writing this is known as a literary device. More precisely, writing from an alternate point-of-view. Which is exactly what we want to do here.

Empathy is an easy word to say. But do we really understand and share the feelings of others? With this exercise we personify that word. If you're having trouble starting then simply write, "I'm angry because…" and take it from there. Go stream of consciousness. Don't lift your pen off the paper. Don't stop typing to think.

Embrace their emotions.

Let go.

Forgive.

Triggers

James Brown

I wish I could say that I got clean and sober the first time I attempted to get clean and sober. I wish I could say that I got clean and sober the second or third or fourth time I attempted to get clean and sober. But it didn't work that way. Call me stupid. Call me weak. Whatever label you want to slap on me, the fact remains that I had a really tough time giving up alcohol and drugs. I'd used and abused for so many years that getting high and drunk was far more natural to me than *not* using and abusing.

Alcohol and drugs were my best friends, or so I thought, because they were always there for me when I needed them most. Stressed? Have a drink. Feeling depressed? Take a pill or snort a line. Feeling happy? I could feel even better if I celebrated with my best friends.

Of course I was lying to myself.

In the beginning, if I took a drink or a drug, I could predict how they'd affect me, and that effect was usually good. But in the later stages of my addiction, when I put booze or drugs into my system, all bets were off. Sure, that initial sweet rush that comes with the first line or the first few drinks was still there, but after that my moods and behavior became unpredictable and erratic. I said and did things I'd never do sober, things that filled me with shame, regret, guilt and remorse, much of which I still carry with me today.

My best friends had turned on me with a vengeance. And yet, when I tried to shake them, they kept reminding me of the good old days when we used to have fun together.

It's called "euphoric recall," and it's just one of a hundred triggers that can lead to a relapse. Admitting you're an alcoholic-addict is the first step in recovery (if you don't believe you have a problem, you certainly can't begin to fix it), but getting clean and sober, and staying clean and sober, are two different matters.

Weathering the early stages of physical withdrawal is a cakewalk compared to the far more vicious battle waged in the mind. Let the mere thought of drinking and using roll around in your head for any amount of time and you're well on your way to a relapse. The obsession to drink or use is our deadliest enemy, and we must, always, be conscious of its presence. Sometimes it's like a ghost, there one second, gone the next, no discernable shape or form. Other times it's standing right in front of us, only our eyes are closed and we don't see it.

The goal of the following exercise is to help us open our eyes.

It's to help us *see*.

In recognizing those people, places or things that might endanger our sobriety we can better protect ourselves from relapsing.

* * *

What I want you to do, in two-to-three pages, is write a scene showing an alcoholic-addict character returning to her neighborhood after being clean and sober for six months.

Describe the neighborhood and what it looks like.

Describe the character, what she looks like, how she walks and talks. Feel free to dip back in time, comparing her looks now to what she looked like six months earlier.

Face bloated as a drunk?

Skeletal-thin as a tweaker?

And tell us about her situation, how she's just gotten out of rehab, or maybe she's been locked up and recently paroled. Is she returning to family? Does she have a kid? Is she nervous about seeing him again?

Whatever the situation, when she arrives home, what sort of triggers does she need to look out for if she wants to keep her sobriety?

What memories does she have that might cause her to think about drinking or using again? What about her friends and relatives? Would one of them tempt her with a drink, a line, a pill? Would others want to throw her a party to celebrate her homecoming?

What about driving by an old bar your character used to drink at, or her old connect's house, or even pushing a cart down the liquor aisle of a grocery store?

Is any of that dangerous?

It was for me.

The list of potential triggers is long and varied. Your job is to show us what she's up against returning home, and the many temptations she'll need to recognize and resist in order to keep her sobriety. It's about vigilance. It's about being hyper-alert to our surroundings, all the hidden landmines, IED's, and snipers just lying-in wait to take you and me out the second we look away.

Play the Tape All the Way Through
Patrick O'Neil

One of the hardest challenges to staying sober is something that Jim already mentioned called "euphoric recall," where your addiction causally tosses you a wonderful memory of getting loaded. Like back in the day when drugs and alcohol were working. You were happy. Getting high was the reprieve from life you so desperately needed. You had finally found the "solution" to all your problems. If you could just stay loaded then everything would be okay. Uh huh, right?

Of course that was before drugs and alcohol became your entire life. Before family, friends, jobs, and responsibilities got in the way of using. Before you started crossing lines you always said you'd never cross. Before all the bad behaviors and dishonesty.

But your addiction doesn't want you to remember any of that "negative" stuff. It wants you to only recall that first good high. The spine-tingling rush of meth as it courses through your veins. That calming warmth from a double shot of scotch. Or the narcotic opiated nod, drifting in and out of reality.

Euphoric recall is a sleight of hand con game on your brain. You know something isn't right. But your craving desires and emotions are getting in the way, and if you let them get to you, you'll act accordingly. Unfortunately with sobriety the stakes are high, and relapse is the inevitable conclusion.

I can remember a particularly difficult time during one of my numerous attempts to get sober. I was in residential rehab, been there about two months, and I was craving drugs so bad I could literally taste them. There was this one really cool counselor and I told him I was thinking of leaving because every moment of the day I was dreaming of getting loaded.

"Play the tape all the way through," was his response.

Which of course sounded cool. But I didn't know what the hell he was talking about. His statement thoroughly confused me.

"You're like someone in an abusive relationship," he explained. "You want to remember all that good sex, but you don't want to remember the violence and pain."

He was right.

The days before I had entered treatment were some of the worst of my life. I only weighed 125 pounds, and I'm 5'10. My face was gaunt and pale. My arms were full of scars. I owed everyone money. No one wanted anything to do with me. None of them trusted me. My parole agent was looking to violate me and send me back to prison. I felt dejected, rejected, lost and alone.

Nothing, and I really mean *nothing*, was going good in my life and I could attribute it all to being strung-out on heroin.

Yet there I was with almost 60 days clean and willing and wanting to throw it all away just to get high again. There is no logic to addiction. It doesn't make sense to people who aren't addicts. In fact a woman at a Q&A after one of my readings asked me, "Why didn't you just stop using before it got so bad?" I was floored by how simplistic she thought addiction was. Just stop? Why hadn't I thought of that?

Unfortunately I had. Hundreds of times I'd white-knuckled it through the pain-filled days of withdrawal just to go back to using as soon as the drugs left my body and the cravings started again.

But I'm getting ahead of myself here. Let's go back to playing the tape all the way through. Instead of letting our addiction fixate on the "good times," let's push fast-forward and run it through to the end where there were plenty of "not-so-good times." By telling the whole story we can eliminate the "euphoria" in the euphoric recall.

Now most novels and stories incorporate what's called a narrative arc, which is the story's full progression. In a simplified version it looks something like A: The Beginning, where the story/conflict originates. Then B: The Middle, where it rises to its peak/climax. And lastly C: The End, where there's resolution (or at least some sort of conclusion).

For us addicts and alcoholics in recovery the narrative arc is pretty simple.

A: Discover drugs and alcohol.

B: Drugs and alcohol become a problem.

C: The addict/alcoholic gets clean and sober.

But for our purposes, with this next exercise, we're only going to be using A & B (the Beginning and Middle), because that's where this study in contrasts really works.

* * *

So get ready. Pen and paper or sitting in front of the keyboard. This is a two-part exercise with the goal of two-to-three pages for each part.

Now for the first part think about your first time(s) using or drinking. Imagine the entire scenario of what transpired. What was your state of mind before and after? What was the emotional impact of the experience? What promises did you make to yourself? How did this "event" change you and your outlook on life?

Write two-to-three pages describing what happened and how you felt. During and afterwards. Don't worry if this sounds like a love letter praising the substance that destroyed your life. After all you gave it everything, right?

Now put that piece of writing away. Let it sit a few days. Actually just ignore it all together.

When you're ready, think about your last day using. What was your frame of mind then? How desperate were you to stop? Emotionally what was going on? What bargains did you make? How had your life changed?

Take your time and write another two-to-three pages. Really dig deep into the emotions, the fear, and desperation.

* * *

When you're finished read them both. Back-to-back. Starting with your first day using, and then your last. This is you playing the tape all the way though. Your words taking you, the addict-alcoholic, from the days when drugs were new and "fun" to the bitter end, whether that's right before seeking sobriety and recovery, or jails, institutions, or death. The allure of the first time in comparison to the last is always a stark contrast and destroys any illusions our memories might have.

When you're done, call someone in recovery, or at least someone who understands addiction. With this kind of explorative writing it's best to do a little self-care afterwards. When we write about drinking and using there are a ton of triggers. Oddly even writing about the "bad days" can be triggering. That's just how treacherous addiction is.

So make sure to take care of yourself.

Close Calls and Narrow Escapes

James Brown

I suffer from Old Professor's Syndrome. It's a condition brought on by teaching the same subjects and classes for decades. The common symptoms include anhedonia, apathy, laziness and good old-fashioned boredom. Severe cases often lead to high rates of absenteeism, a disdain for the teaching profession and one's students, and most frequently early retirement.

Fortunately those who suffer from Old Professor's syndrome don't exhibit all these symptoms, and though I count myself among the less seriously afflicted, I am nonetheless guilty of sometimes feeling bored out of my mind.

To rectify, or better yet, *mollify* my disinterest in the subject matter I often deviate from my lectures by telling stories unrelated to the curriculum. Many of my students enjoy my digressions, or at least they say as much in the end-of-the-term instructor evaluations, while others complain that I ought to stay on track and teach what I'm supposed to teach. Let the complainers complain. Such are the pleasures of tenure.

I've paid my dues, and in my pea-brain I can find connections in literature that somehow, some way always relates back to human excesses, flaws, virtues and short-comings. After all isn't that what literature is really about? And if we're talking about the authors themselves, well, alcoholism seems more the norm than the exception.

But, as in class, I digress.

The story I want to tell is the story I often serve up to my students in the form of a Personal Public Service Announcement to the budding alcoholics and addicts seated before me and all those, and there are many, who have alcoholic-addict parents, siblings or friends.

I tell them I shouldn't be alive.

I tell them that there was a time when I thought I drove better drunk than sober because my nerves, like my shaky hands, were steadier after a few drinks. And I tell them that years ago, if I had to teach an evening class, that it nearly killed me. If I didn't have a drink by a certain hour (typically before 4 p.m. but absolutely no later than 5), my blood pressure soared, my heart sped up, my hands trembled, my face turned bright red and I'd begin to sweat heavily.

Not surprisingly I let my evening classes out at least 30 minutes early. No answering questions after class. No office hours. I packed up my things and got the hell out of there, jumped in my car and rushed to the closest liquor store to campus. The clerk knew me so well that as soon as I entered the store he'd set a half-pint of Smirnoff Blue Label on the counter, the hundred-proof stuff, while I hurried to the coolers for a Tall Boy of their most potent malt liquor.

In the parking lot, I'd take the cap off the half-pint and throw it in the trashcan because it wasn't going back on that bottle. Three swallows and it was gone. In a minute, my hands stopped shaking, my heartbeat returned to normal, and the sweating stopped.

Now I could safely operate heavy machinery.

As for the malt liquor, I cradled that between my legs as I drove, nursing it until I got to the next liquor store, the one closest to home.

The students, when I tell this story, look dumbstruck, and I know what they're thinking.

This is my *professor*?

Yeah, that's me, or that *was* me. There's a second leg to the story, but I have to flash-forward to tell it. In this part I'm closing in on 90 days of sobriety when the academic quarter begins. It's fall. I accumulated the sober time over the summer when I didn't have to teach and could concentrate on my recovery without the pressures of school and teaching and department politics. But now those relatively stress-free days were over, and there I was again, having to teach another evening class.

The first week wasn't too bad stress-wise because it's mostly about going over the syllabus, taking attendance, and having the students introduce themselves to the class, what they're majoring in, their career plans, that sort of thing. But by the second and third week we're digging into the assigned readings, the papers start coming in, the workload picks up, and the anxiety levels rise. And handling anxiety isn't the strong suit of the alcoholic-addict, especially one wrestling with recovery.

So it's back to the five o'clock jitters, only it's not the sweating, shaky hands and rapid heartbeat. I passed through the physical withdrawals during the first 10 or so days after taking my last drink nearly three months before. These jitters are in the mind and they're just as real as the physical.

By the time class is over, my nerves are shot, and I don't want to drive to the liquor store, but my car is on autopilot and it takes me straight there.

I park.

I go inside. It's the same clerk, and though it's been a while since I've seen him, his memory is sharp. He puts a half-pint of Smirnoff Blue Label on the counter as I head to the coolers for a Tall Boy of malt liquor. I pay him. But instead of opening the vodka and downing it in the parking lot, I take it and Tall Boy back to the car with me. I just sit there. I don't open the paper bag.

All sorts of thoughts run through my head.

Do I want to blow almost 90 days? I was looking forward to taking my chip and hearing everyone clap and congratulate me at my A.A. meeting. And, shit, I'd hate to have to tell my sponsor that I slipped. Again. Because this was hardly the first time. But wouldn't that wonderful vodka burning its way down my throat and shooting into my bloodstream feel so good? All that tension and anxiety gone in a minute, two at most. And then that nice warm fuzzy feeling filling me up. Damn, how I missed it.

So what did I do?

This is where my story becomes yours.

I want you to create a character like me in this same precarious situation. Or if you prefer, if you've had a similar experience, write it as it happened to you.

* * *

In two-to-three pages, write about what's running through your mind or your character's as she sits in her car with an unopened bottle of booze. Or, if you're a dope fiend, create a character (or let it be yourself) who's just left the dealer's house with a bindle of meth or coke or heroin or whatever other poison you prefer. (I know, I know, we usually hang out a while and test the product before we leave the dope man's place, if only for their own protection; people constantly coming and going at all hours of the night is like placing a flashing neon sign in the window saying *Dope House*, *Dope House*; but, once again, I digress.)

Either way the person you're writing about is in the car and the booze or dope is right there with her and she has a decision to make, possibly a life and death decision, because we don't always come back from our slips.

One sip from that bottle and you know there's no stopping.

One line, one shot, and you'll be craving more even before the magic wears off. You don't get to get high or drunk just this once, just one last time, though you may well tell yourself exactly that.

In your head or the character's, go back and forth between the truth and lies we tell ourselves to justify what we know, deep down, is a huge mistake.

Wrestle with the demons.

Go toe-to-toe with the enemy. Bite. Scratch. Choke him out. It's a no-holds barred fight. All is fair in love and war, they say, and this is a war against our mistaken love for the very thing that wants to kill us.

But there is one rule.

I want your story to end as mine did that night.

I want you or your character to make the right decision, even if, in your own life, in a situation like this or one similar, you personally did not.

This time I want you to come out on top.

We need to beat the monster together, so that my experience becomes yours if only through the eyes of an imaginary character. And in this case, on that perilous night long ago, that bottle of Smirnoff went right where it belonged — in the trashcan with the cap still on it.

The "R" Word
Patrick O'Neil

Even though Jim and I have already dipped your toes in this torrid pool, I'd still like to take another run at this subject. It's not only uncomfortable and rife for exploratory writing, but also prevalent and foremost on everyone's mind. You know it as the "boogeyman" of recovery. The BIG "R." That relentless bad thing lurking in the background, ready to pounce at a moment's notice when the addict's program is slipping, or the alcoholic is out socializing and drinks are being served. It's the number one topic at most 12-Step meetings, and even people with decades of time are not immune to its lure.

Relapse!

While I'm being slightly facetious on a very serious subject it is still safe to say that relapse is one of *the* most devastating things that can happen to a person in recovery. Not only is their life in jeopardy (it's not always a given that we'll come back from a relapse), but it's usually accompanied by overpowering feelings of failure, a prevailing sense of weakness, and a shit-ton of guilt and shame (and let's not forget all the not so helpful judgmental opinions that other folks might heap on us as an extra helping of their disappointment, scorn, and mistrust).

However, relapse can also be one of the most "educational" experiences that any of us will ever live through. I know that sounds awfully "glass half full," but it's the truth. The support from the fellowship alone is tremendously eye opening and empowering. But the insights one can gain are a much needed and vital dose of reality, allowing us to see (in real time) what we are, and are not doing, to keep and maintain our sobriety.

The "official" understanding of relapse is that it happens way before we pick up a drink or a drug. Usually for those in the fellowship our meeting attendance starts to slip, we stop calling our sponsors, or the job we found in sobriety suddenly becomes our main focus and we're too busy for anything else. This is not to say that all of these may happen over time, and here and there, but relapse usually follows a pattern that predates us magically discovering a drink in our hand.

Then there's life just showing up and if we're not vigilant we can be woefully unprepared to deal with it. Stuff like relationships, death of a loved one, finances, our mental health, insane family, or even success can all be so overwhelming that the idea of checking out just seems like the only viable response.

The cold hard truth is that for us drug addicts and alcoholics, using is our natural state; sobriety is our unnatural state. And because it is, we have to really work hard to stay sober.

Which, 20 years ago, I thought I was doing. But with my last relapse I really didn't have a program of recovery and it was devastating.

It was my second time in treatment and I had just completed a year and a half in a behavior modification residential rehab. Which, if you are not familiar with it, is not your 12-Step based recovery. It's the exact opposite. With behavior modification they tear you down mentally, addressing all your ingrained bad behaviors, selfish thoughts, and internalized anger. Mostly they achieve this by just screaming at you and telling you that you're a loser and a fuck up. Both of which at that point in my life were sadly not news to me.

It's grueling, rough, and in your face. Like boot camp for drug addicts that have never obeyed the rules or had structure in their lives. At the very least we were forced to really look at who we were. How our behaviors and beliefs had affected everything and those around us. The theory is that if you address and fix these issues then drugs and alcohol will no longer be needed.

Unfortunately that program's game plan was to have you sign up for life and never leave. But at 18 months they give you the option to tap out. Thinking I still had a life out there I wanted to live instead of living it for the program, I left. At that moment if you had asked me if I were "cured" I would have told you that I was never going to use heroin again.

Because I really thought I was done.

Fast-forward to a year later, I had the job, the apartment, the girlfriend, a bank account, and my first credit card. By all outward appearances I'd made it out of my addiction and into the real world.

Then one night my girlfriend and I were at a swank restaurant, one whose trademark specialty was oversized six-ounce martinis (see, there's already a foreseeable problem here). But you know, our lives were great and we were out celebrating.

Before we had even ordered our food a waitress walked by with a tray full of said martinis and my mouth watered. I could visualize the cool condensation on the glasses, the cold vodka and vermouth sloshing inside, a toothpick pierced olive doing a swirly dance, inviting me to indulge.

"Hey, let's have a drink," I suggested. "We've been good. What could it hurt?"

Three martinis later and we're drunk. Like shitfaced.

In the morning I'm hungover. I hadn't had a drink or a drug in two and half years. I'm feeling the shame. I curse myself for being a failure. My girlfriend is crying. We've lost our sobriety and now we have to fess-up to our friends and family or lie and pretend it never happened.

Now I don't want to get bogged down with the natural progression of this relapse, but I'm pretty sure you all know how it ends. No matter how many times I told myself I was okay, it was just a slip, at least it wasn't heroin, alcohol is not my drug of choice, and blah, blah, blah, I had awoken the beast. And suddenly I'm hiding secrets, being sneaky and dishonest.

With no program of recovery and a massive craving building up inside of me I eventually found myself knocking on the dope man's door. And the rest, as they say, is history.

I went from using that one time (because that's what I told myself I was doing), to three times a day, and with the same addictive urgency I had before I quit. I lost the apartment because my money went to buy drugs instead. The relationship fell apart; I was fired from my job for not showing up half the time, and worst of all I absconded from parole because I couldn't pass the piss test. Without exaggerating I can say with all certainty that I had totally destroyed my life and found myself at square one again.

Now this relapse didn't happen because I was weak willed, or intentionally looking for an excuse to get loaded, or I was a bad person that just didn't deserve good things in life (all of which I told myself were true). What it really came down to was what I wasn't doing before that fateful dinner out.

I wasn't going to meetings. I didn't have a support system. I wasn't active in my recovery. And while I was abstaining from using, I was still me. Bad behaviors and all.

Months earlier I had begun padding my hours at work because... well, I worked hard damn it, those people owed me more money. A few times I stopped by the old haunts to visit friends I knew were still using, just to see how they were doing, as if I didn't know. And at the local grocery store, after strolling down the liquor aisle as if window-shopping (look, a new brand of vodka!), I shoplifted a thing or two... oh yeah, old habits die hard.

Without actually using I was straddling the line between addiction and sobriety, with the occasional subconscious sidestep to test the water should I want to go all the way. Which of course happened that night in the swank restaurant. Had I known what I was doing I could've been more prepared. But I wasn't. Woefully ill-equipped and clueless the big "R" had kicked my ass.

Now if you're sober, in recovery, or working a program, then this next exercise may feel counterproductive, illogical, or even destructive. But...

* * *

What I'm going to ask you to do is write out your relapse (or your fictional character's relapse) in four-to-five pages. Go as far back pre-relapse as you want. But just get us from where it all started going south to the actual using and drinking. Plan it out. Give us the details. Expose the sneaky behaviors. The denial. The lies. The justifications. Then the actual act and what that felt like.

This can tie into Jim's assignment for the "Close Calls and Narrow Escapes" chapter where you were asked to write about what's running through the addict or alcoholic's mind, where you "wrestle with the demons," as they say, or you are just about to take that first hit of dope, or a sip off the bottle. But instead of making the right decision, you go full rogue and relapse. If you want to take it further, follow through with the repercussive aftermath. It's your call. However, I'm suggesting that you write at least four pages. Because I want the full story. I don't want you to gloss over the details.

* * *

So, what's the point?" you may be asking. "How the hell is this going to help me stay sober?"

At first glance it may look and feel like I'm encouraging you to go out and drink and use. But what I'm suggesting is the exact opposite. You know where the drugs and booze are. It's not like I'm exposing a magic trick and now the slight-of-hand illusion won't work anymore. Whether we want to admit it or not, we're conniving, manipulative, dishonest addicts and alcoholics. And although we may not be consciously aware of it, in the back of our minds there is always a plan. Even if it's just as simple as I don't want to feel this anymore and I know what works to stop these feelings.

I can't tell you how many times in early recovery I overindulged in food, caffeine, sex, or exercise in the hopes of altering my mind. I desperately wanted to not feel what I was feeling, but without drugs and alcohol the euphoric reprieve of a benign substance or behavior was short lived at best.

By tapping into our subconscious plan we can reveal a whole lot about ourselves. And believe it or not this is what a relapse prevention plan starts to look like. When the cravings start, or when using seems like a good idea, pull out this assignment and read it again. It's not a happy ending. But it could be what stops you from going all the way.

It's Not Just About You
(And It Never Was)
James Brown

I cringe when I think about all the people I've hurt. Everyone has said and did things that they regret, but chances are, if you're an alcoholic-addict, you've done a whole lot more damage than your ordinary run-of-the-mill jerk. We're especially good at screwing up not just our own lives but also those of the ones we love most — husbands and wives, sons and daughters, fathers and mothers, grandparents, uncles and aunts and our closest friends. Basically, we're bound to have hurt anyone who ever cared about us.

But it's not personal.

It's not as if we set out to cause grief and pain and despair to our loved ones. It's not as if, when we first started drinking and taking drugs, that we intended to ruin our marriages and relationships and traumatize our children, husbands, wives and partners.

Addiction is considered a selfish disease, and once it has a hold on us, all we can focus on is that next drink, that next fix. The obsession consumes us, utterly and entirely, and God help the person who gets in our way. And God help the person who has to deal with our hangovers and withdrawals when our emotions and moods spin out of control, raging one second, crying the next. Our tantrums. Our fits. All that meanness and madness born of addiction.

But that's not us. Not the real us, anyway.

It's the addiction talking.

It's the addiction driving our ugly behavior. I believe that, but what I believe doesn't make the damage we do any less harmful. Nor is it an excuse. Addiction or not, we still have to own up to our actions and take responsibility for them.

Alcoholic-addicts are experts at self-pity. We're also wonderfully proficient in feeling guilty and making worthless promises and apologies. I'm a specialist in the use of the word *sorry*, but after saying it ten thousand times, for some strange reason, it seems to lose its meaning. We wear it out. We wear people down, and until we can clean up our act and take a step back and look at ourselves, we can't begin to understand what we've put others through with our addiction.

But even that's not enough.

We need to be able to *see through the eyes of those we've hurt*. We need, to the best of our abilities, to *become* that other person. We need to *think* like them. We need to *feel* what they felt and the best way to do that is by putting ourselves in their place. Embracing the consciousness of a loved one, real or invented, is bound to give us a greater sense of empathy and compassion for them.

This next exercise is similar to Patrick's "Forgive Us Our Sins, Or Something Along Those Lines" in that it asks you to assume the persona of someone you've hurt. Although both are designed to gain a better understanding of others, mine isn't focused on forgiveness. It's broader in scope but I like to think no less important. Besides, it's not like we only hurt one person, and this gives you another opportunity to explore the mind of yet another casualty of our addiction.

* * *

So I want you to write two-or-three pages from the point-of-view of someone who loves an alcoholic-addict.

The alcoholic-addict doesn't have to be you. At the same time, chances are, it'll be based on you because you are the very thing you're writing about. But I want you to mix it up, change names and personal descriptions, maybe write the character as a man if you're a woman, or vice-versa.

As for the loved one's point-of-view, maybe it's the brother of the alcoholic-addict.

Maybe it's the mother.

Maybe it's a sister or father or best friend or husband or wife or significant other. It doesn't matter. It just has to be somebody special, somebody who cares about the alcoholic-addict, and whose life has been adversely affected by this person.

In this scenario, the alcoholic-addict could be locked up. Or he's in rebab. Or he's a kid who's run away from home. Or, far worse, he recently died from an OD. Or maybe you have another idea in mind? Go for it. Just make sure it fits with the rest of the assignment.

Place the loved one in the alcoholic-addict's bedroom. Maybe it's her mom and she's simply sitting on the bed and looking around the room. Something on the dresser triggers a memory. A picture? A special ring or necklace?

What of the poster on the wall?

Or an old CD collection? Does she sift through it? Does one spark a memory? Is it something the alcoholic-addict used to play over and over and that drove her mother crazy? Or what if she got up from the bed and opened the closet or a dresser drawer? What might she find that would trigger more memories and thoughts?

Or what if instead of a mother, it's a husband or wife sitting on the bed?

What we're after here, scene-wise, are details that help define the nature and personality of the person who occupied the room (personal belongings, articles of clothing, etc.) and that simultaneously elicit feelings, thoughts and emotions in the person looking at, holding or touching these belongings.

Again, the perimeters are that the scene is set in a bedroom, it's from the point-of-view of a loved one, and the alcoholic-addict isn't physically present.

The entire exercise takes place inside the character's head as she remembers things about the alcoholic-addict, who he was and what he was like *before* he got strung out, and who he was and what he was like *after* drugs and alcohol took him down.

I could easily see the mother or father, or whoever you want it to be, break down and cry.

I could easily see them blaming themselves, wondering what they did wrong, where they went wrong.

Could they have done more? Was everything their fault?

* * *

When we screw up our lives, the people who love us often blame themselves. My brother and sister were both alcoholics who killed themselves and I spent most of my life wondering what I could've done, should've done, if somehow I might've been able to save them. So it's not hard for me to picture someone else blaming themselves for something they didn't have much if any power over.

What we're after here is the sort of insight that can only be found by stepping back and looking at ourselves through a pair of eyes other than our own.

IT'S NOT JUST ABOUT YOU

We need to use our imaginations.

We need to invent to see beyond the narrow confines of the self. In assuming another persona, we'll better understand how our addiction and reckless behavior impacts those we love. This is potentially a sad, heartbreaking lesson in humility, but we can't hide from it any more than we can our own reflection in the mirror.

How Can You Tell When a Junkie Is Lying?

Patrick O'Neil

We've already talked about the reality of what our addiction and alcoholism really looked like, even if at times we may have tried to dress it up as something else. In our minds we were just getting loaded and not hurting anyone but ourselves. Once we got sober we realized that wasn't quite the truth. Even if we didn't outright perpetrate a crime or directly harm others, our actions still affected everyone else in our lives.

Addiction creates a barrier that makes us unable to be present for anyone or anything. Our self-centered needs of wanting and using more are all we can see.

Consequently our relationships suffer. Responsibilities have less meaning. Dishonesty becomes the norm.

Mostly we were lying by omission. You know that old adage "Don't ask, don't tell," as if our alcoholism was on a need-to-know-only basis. Then again when someone did directly ask if we had a drug problem, nine times out of ten what came out of our mouths wasn't exactly the whole truth.

Alcoholics and addicts are masters of the art of deception. Many of us lie for the sake of lying, even when we could have told a truth. Lying had become so ingrained that it became our default response.

How can you tell when a junkie is lying? Their lips are moving.

Etched in my memory is an extremely difficult encounter with my mother. After my girlfriend took a deliberate overdose of drugs and alcohol with the intent to commit suicide, my mother drove her to the hospital. As my girlfriend had started to fade out, she realized that she didn't want to die and called the only responsible person in our lives (and the only one that owned a car that actually ran). On the way to the ER she told my mother that we had been heroin addicts for years, which was definitely news to my mom.

Later that day I returned home to find a very angry mom in my apartment. She of course knew that I smoked and drank too much, but in her world those were somewhat acceptable. Drug addicts, especially junkies, were not.

"Your girlfriend told me everything."

"What do you mean, Mom?"

"Said you guys have been doing heroin. For Christ's sake, Patrick, heroin?"

"I don't know what she told you. But if you haven't noticed she's a little out of her mind right now."

"I don't think she's making this up."

"So you believe her instead of me. That's great, Mom. You don't even believe your own son."

"I just know what I've seen, and you two haven't been doing so well."

"Things have been kinda hard lately. I'm outta work. I'm depressed, and yeah, I use drugs once in a while. Like, recreationally, you know? But I ain't no junkie."

I am not proud of that conversation. As a matter of fact it makes me shudder just to retell it. In typical junkie fashion I took no responsibility and even threw my girlfriend under the bus. This could have been the moment I came clean and asked for help. My life was a mess. My girlfriend had just attempted suicide. But at that very moment all I could think of was how do I manipulate my way out of this and where the hell was my next hit of dope coming from.

Just like lying is a product of our addiction, honesty is one of the cornerstones of recovery. If you don't agree then just look at all that Step work around admitting our part and then of course making amends for every one of our wrongs. And this brings us to the next writing exercise. Which is exploring the damage and emotional outcome of lies when we tell and/or receive them.

As we all well know lies can be highly traumatic. Deception can be very harmful. The discovery of dishonesty can be the worst of all.

Lies involve two parts: intent and deceit. Liars make a deliberate decision to distort reality and to conceal their motives. Everyone has told a "small" lie. Whether it was for "good" (the "I don't want to hurt you" clause), or to avoid conflict. Often "small" lies backfire and when discovered can cause more damage than the truth.

Small lies can also evolve into the telling of bigger lies to cover up the dishonesty. When the lies pile up the liar eventually builds a false version of reality that distances them from their real selves. Or worse, may even come to believe their lies are the truth.

For lack of a better word, "big" lies are much more involved with intent and deceit. It is an attempt at trickery to make the victim believe in a falsehood. The motivations are numerous and definitely not "noble" in cause as a small lie might be.

* * *

Now for this exercise I'd like you to set a goal of writing three-to-four pages. But first I want you to think of a time when you, or someone else, told a lie. Really look inward and remember the moment and all that surrounded it. When you have it as a total picture in your mind:

Write the lie.
Write who was involved.
Write who was affected.
Write why it was told (if you know).
Write if the lie was ever discovered.
Write if the liar/you were ever confronted.

Write what emotions were evoked.

Write what it would have been like if the lie had never been told.

Using the above suggestions, write about this episode in your life, those involved, the effects, and outcome. Use your emotions to influence your prose.

It can be a lie you told, or a lie that was told to you. And because we are also talking about making up stories that we tell ourselves, you can write the exercise using that premise. This should be a fairly involved exercise. After all the lies we've told in our addiction it shouldn't be that difficult to dig right in. The only difficulty might be in deciding which lie to use. But it's up to you as to how intensely you want to excavate.

And remember, with writing about subjects such as this, it is almost impossible to make ourselves look good or come out unscathed. Just write the truth and you'll be okay.

Finding Your Inner Childish Asshole

James Brown

I'm good at spotting childish assholes. Over the years I've become so skilled at it that I've created three categories of childish assholes: major childish assholes, average childish assholes, and minor childish assholes, hereafter referred to simply as major, average, and minor assholes.

Major assholes are so easily recognizable that they need no formal introduction. Your average asshole, however, is a classification that comprises the bulk of assholes, namely those people who feel compelled to say shitty things to and about others in, for instance, A.A. meetings, or by trolling their victims on Facebook and Twitter. These ones also regularly cut you off on the road and give you the finger. Lastly, there is the minor asshole. Those in this class know when they're being jerks and often try not to be, but for some reason they just can't seem to help themselves. There's hope for the minor asshole. There's hope for the average, run-of-the-mill asshole, too. But the major asshole? His is an uphill battle that requires much self-examination and reflection in order to change, and in some cases the condition is terminal.

Of course I'm not judging anyone, especially by something so superficial as looks. The guy with the tats and scraggily goatee, his Nikes untied and baggy pants sagging off his ass isn't a member of a lower species. The girl in the short-shorts and coming out of her top isn't insecure and trying to get attention. And the vain older guy in the tight T-shirt isn't anything like me, trying to show off his muscles.

I don't know if it's human nature to pass judgment on others, if it's our ego getting the best of us, or if we're making a pathetic attempt to feel better about our own failings at another's expense, but I'm definitely guilty of it.

In A.A., judging others is considered a character flaw, right up there with the Seven Deadly Sins of Pride, Greed, Lust, Envy, Gluttony, Anger and Sloth. I would score my asshole quotient in the major category, particularly when it comes to feeling superior to my alcoholic-addict brothers and sisters. Sometimes when someone shares a story at a meeting that little voice in my head says "that fool is such a loser he'll never get sober" or "that jerk is so full of himself it's no wonder his wife left him." I also resent the old timers with decades of sobriety browbeating newcomers when they're bearing their souls by cutting them off and shutting them down with their sage advice.

I once witnessed a self-righteous old timer tell an emotionally fragile young woman in her first 48 hours of sobriety that she didn't belong in the meeting because she introduced herself as an "addict" rather than an "alcoholic" and she rushed out of the room in tears. I hurried after her but she jumped into her car and raced off before I could catch her. She never came back, either.

What a fucker, I thought of that old timer, and I told him so at the break. He called me an arrogant bastard, I called him something just as bad, and after that we never said another word to each other. It was all anger and dirty looks. About a year later he moved to Thailand and last I heard he "hired" a 13-year-old girl to take care of him. You can figure out the twisted details on your own.

Nonetheless, in A.A. resentment is considered the "number one" offender, causing more alcoholics to relapse than any other emotion, and there we were, putting our sobriety at risk along with our spiritual and mental health because of a beef over a young woman who needed help. He was a jerk, sure, but then what did that make me?

Even if I could call my intentions noble and his cruel, that old timer and I still weigh-in close to the same on the Richter scale of assholeishness. We're both in the major category for keeping our grudge alive and well, recycling and reliving negative feelings every time we saw each other.

So here's what I want you to do.

You're going to be an asshole. Or rather you're going to create one, which shouldn't be too hard given that we all have a little or a lot of asshole in us, and those who believe they're asshole-free are most likely head-to-toe full of it.

Assholes can be spotted in any number of ways, including how they might dress, how they might walk, wear their hair or carry themselves, but generally speaking labeling someone an asshole solely by the way they look is neither fair nor adequate. Capturing the true nature of a real asshole is best accomplished by rendering them in action, *showing* us what they say or do and to whom.

There is the pious asshole.

You'll see them in A.A. as the holier-than-thou type, lecturing the less spiritually enlightened among us. Instead of saying "I," restricting their profound insights to their own experiences when addressing the group, they'll say "we" or "you," and make plentiful use of terms like "should" and "must." Like religious zealots, they want to impose their beliefs on others, rather than offer them up as suggestions. They also love to quote the Big Book by chapter and verse as evidence of their divine wisdom.

Then you have the victim types who blame everyone but themselves for their addiction and personal problems. They like to moan and groan about how unfair life is, how badly the world has treated them, and some frequently resort to tears to gain the group's sympathy. I know I'm being a little harsh with this type, but if they don't break the cycle of victimhood and take responsibility for their actions, they'll invariably find a lame excuse to drink or use again.

Another type of major asshole often takes the form of the younger alcoholic-addict whose mommy and daddy have spent their life savings and hocked their home to send little Johnny or Jane countless times to cushy luxury rehabs from Malibu to Hawaii and they still don't get it, let alone seem to care.

Am I being judgmental?

Absolutely, and now it's your turn to do the same.

* * *

In two-to-three pages, I want you to assume the voice and character of a major asshole.

I want you to write it in the form of a dramatic monologue, which is a long speech by one person, broken up in spots with gestures, movements and pauses. Those gestures and movements are the details of body-language, and body-language speaks volumes about a person's moods, feelings, thoughts and character. It also adds authenticity to the monologue, because in real life we don't sit completely still, only working our mouths, when we talk for more than a sentence or two. Anything longer and we might wave our hands, bite our lip, blink, clench our teeth, make a face, raise or lower our voice, maybe pound the table if we're angry, or scratch our head if we're puzzled about something.

Or you could do what's called in literary jargon a dramatic *interior* monologue, which is another long speech, only it all takes place in the head. An internal conversation within the character's mind. The thoughts might be linear and easy to follow or they could take the form of a stream of consciousness, replicating the experience of our sometimes chaotic, jumpy, disjointed way of thinking.

As for the character, they should be an alcoholic-addict. The main point behind the assignment is to better recognize ourselves and our own assholeishness in relation to the character we create and what we might share in common with them. Only you'll know what those connections may or may not be, because this stuff is made up, billed as fiction, freeing you to write whatever you want about anybody you want with complete impunity.

The alcoholic-addict character should be someone who sorely lacks insight into their deeply flawed self, and, as a result, has earned the title of major asshole. We as readers, we as outsiders, can see in the character what the character can't see in themselves, be it selfishness, pride, laziness or any of the other Seven Deadly Sins. And I bet you'll catch more than a glimpse of yourself in the process.

The setting could be an A.A. meeting, but it doesn't have to be.

You could have your character driving, just thinking to himself, and by his thoughts alone show him for the misguided soul he is.

You could have him tailgating some nervous and scared old woman who can't see the road well, honking at her, maybe flipping her off.

In, say, the A.A. meeting, your two-to-three pages could be an entire monologue of someone sharing their story, and sharing it in such a way as to suggest that they have some serious personal responsibility issues.

Or you could write it from the point-of-view of the A.A. guru.

Or the ungrateful younger alcoholic-addict.

Or what about the ranting of an angry parent who doesn't understand the first thing about her child's addiction?

Or how about an interior monologue from a burned-out drug and alcohol counselor who's sick and tired of working with junkies and drunks and listening to all their poor-me sob stories?

In short, write about any character you want, whether it's a borderline facsimile of yourself or someone entirely out of the orbit of your personal experience. The only one off limits is that arrogant old timer who "hired" a 13-year-old girl in Thailand to take care of him. I'm keeping him all to myself to judge, if God already hasn't. There's a special place in hell for a man like that.

Writing Through the Wreckage of Our Past

Patrick O'Neil

As writers of memoirs what Jim and I essentially do is chronicle the worst moments of our lives and then share them very publicly with strangers. Similarly with some of our personal essays and articles we tap into those same experiences as a way of personalizing the subject matter. As if to say, "Hey I've walked the walk, I [hopefully] know what I'm talking about." And here with this book we're doing more of the same.

Now one would think that over the span of our careers that writing about addiction and the challenging aftermath of dealing with the consequences would have become easier. Unfortunately, at least for me, that isn't always so.

I'm not proud of a great deal of my past and I know that Jim isn't either. I carry a lot of guilt and shame, and remembering, reliving and divulging certain memories in order to write about them can be an intense and demanding struggle.

Likewise some of you may have experienced similar reactions when faced with the writing exercises Jim and I have presented in this book. For the majority we've asked you to really dig in, get honest, examine your past, confront negative behaviors and thinking, and begin to address some extremely difficult subjects that were probably more than uncomfortable to look at. Let alone write about.

Jim and I realize that this is a huge undertaking, but we also know from experience that it's an undertaking worth doing. Even if it's still a struggle every goddamn time you sit down to write. If you want to work through your unresolved resentments, that overwhelming sense of guilt, or those persistent fears — especially the ones that you've been denying and avoiding — then writing about them is an excellent tool to begin the process.

Plus, for us writers of memoir, we're not going to be able to write that really kick-ass book until we

THE WRECKAGE OF OUR PAST

come to some understanding with our past. Readers can sense when we haven't put in the work to move on, or found self-forgiveness, or at the very least some form of acceptance.

I can't tell you how many times I've started reading a recovery memoir only to discover that the author is seriously conflicted as to whether they should be proud of screwing up, angry at having to get sober, stoked they're not drinking, or remorseful for all the damage they've done. And most times, if they don't know, then I don't care enough to finish reading their work.

Also, from a purely structural point of view, at some point your writing will always lead you back to the parts of your life that you just don't want to write about and you'll be stuck staring at this big uncomfortable gap in your story.

Which brings to mind another quote that is often mangled and overused in the rooms of recovery, "no matter where you go, there you are." In other words, there's just no getting away from ourselves. However when we deal with the things we don't want to deal with then we're getting that much closer to a place where we can begin to heal.

In recovery "they" call it cleaning up the wreckage of our past. I think of it as dealing with all the fucked-up things I did and that were done to me. But labeling it in a term that makes more sense doesn't make the writing any easier. There's going to be bumps in the road. You will get emotional, depressed, and wrought with anxiety. It's going to suck. I know that might not sound like a lot of fun, and I don't want to discourage anyone from writing their story, but it's the truth.

I can remember back when I was a fledgling writer and being super excited that I was finally starting my first memoir. There I'd be all set up at my desk, fingers on the keyboard, words flowing, and everything going along smoothly. You know, in that awesome writing groove that we all love when it's happening. And then the "story" would eventually lead me to a really uncomfortable and hard-to-write area. And it would be like slamming into a brick wall, stopping my happy little writing groove dead in its tracks.

Unable to go any further I'd berate myself for not being a good enough writer, or think I just didn't have the ability to capture the severity of the situation, or I'd tell myself those memories weren't that important.

But what I wasn't taking into consideration was the sheer intensity of those memories. What I'm talking about are the memories I avoid because they are really painful. The ones that cause a physical reaction where I would actually shudder, or hold my breath, or my stomach would torque up in knots. Those memories are a much different animal than the embarrassing memories, or the stressful, sad, and anxiety ridden ones you don't want anyone to know about because of the shame and guilt and you're afraid they'll judge you.

No, the memories I'm referring to here are the ones that would be labeled as traumatic.

Such as a particularly violent memory I have from prison where I can still see the hatred and intense looks on the faces of my assailants. The slow-motion tangled dance of bodies in a physical altercation. An adrenaline rush of fight-or-flight, with nowhere to go, but a powerful determination to survive. I'm in a dimly lit corridor, my back against the wall, defense wounds on both arms, and my blood splayed across the gray cement floor. Afterwards the detached uncaring expression of a very bored nurse as she sewed me up without anesthesia.

Yet even though I'm able to recall all those vivid details and essentially relive the emotions that are attached to that memory, it is still very disjointed. There are parts that are vague, and parts that feel like I'm getting hit with a baseball bat. My unspoken rationale is I just don't want to deal with it. I'd rather forget this ever happened. And because of all that I've stuffed it deep down inside, hoping it would somehow miraculously go away.

Consequently getting stabbed in prison is not something I often talk about (not exactly dinner party conversation). But for many years afterwards the corresponding anger and fear were always there, just below the surface, a feral reaction waiting to happen whenever the hint of violence was in the air.

Films and TV shows with graphic violence could sometimes trigger that reaction. So would aggressive angry people and confining dark spaces. Yet it wasn't like I would consciously react to these things. It was more like re-experiencing that same surge of fight or flight adrenaline. Then feeling extremely uncomfortable and confused. Because it felt like I was overreacting.

When I talked to a behavioral therapist about what was happening she patiently explained that our brains save and code traumatic memories differently then non-traumatic memories. Mainly because the original experience causes super high levels of anxiety, adrenaline, and duress. And then when something causes us to remember that experience all that gets activated again, generating a similar response — think overwhelming fear, revulsion, guilt, and shame.

I can honestly tell you that for me that memory does all the above. Do I wish it had never happened? Of course I do. But I can't change the fact that it did. It's forever stored away in my brain and my only recourse is to stay in denial and somehow avoid remembering it. Or work through it and find some sort of acceptance for a horrific situation that wasn't my fault.

Now I'd like to think I've done the latter, even though I've only written about it once (before now), and that piece never saw the light of day. However, to be totally transparent, I didn't write it for general consumption. I wrote it as an exercise similar to the one I've created for this chapter.

Although I can totally admit that my first intention was to just get that memory down into words and then be finished with it in order to move on. But then that process morphed into wanting a better understanding of how trauma works, and in turn I learned how to dissect the hell out of that memory and see it for what it was: *violence done onto me in a very violent world*. And I was able to find some acceptance with what happened; *I couldn't prevent the assault, it wasn't my fault, but my actions had put me in that environment, and those were the consequences.*

Armed with that understanding, while continuing to engage in my internal recovery work (Step work, sponsorship, and meetings), I can honestly say that this memory no longer holds the same emotional weight it once did and I was able to finally find some acceptance and resolution with my past.

Okay, so enough about me and my old traumatic memories. *Yikes, all he does is talk about himself* (laughs). Let's talk about your traumatic memories. The ones that evoke that same visceral response I previously described. The dark secrets you said you'd never tell. Memories so shrouded in guilt and shame you've shoved them deep inside never to be let out.

That's the stuff we're going to be writing about.

However I first want to preface this by saying that trauma isn't a contest of who had the worst thing happen to them. What may be traumatic to you might not be to me, and vice versa. Yet the trap we fall into is that we tell ourselves we shouldn't be traumatized because there are those that have had it worse (*I didn't get shanked in prison like he did*). Only if that were true, why are we still haunted by these memories?

Now I'm not a licensed therapist or psychiatrist so what I'm encouraging you to do with this next exercise isn't a substitute for getting professional help. However just like with the Step work of A.A. (or any other "A") writing can be a very effective "therapeutic" tool. The word "cathartic" is often cited as a result when writing about trauma. But I think the poet Rainer Maria Rilke said it best, "The work of the eyes is done. Go now and do the heart-work on the images imprisoned within you."

* * *

For this exercise let's set our sights on writing four-to-six pages. We've already somewhat established what a traumatic memory is. So this is where you dig deep and take a good look at the memories that you feel are traumatic. They can be anything from a solitary incident to an extended period of your life. However, it is a memory that you find traumatic and that interpretation is personal and yours. Because as I have already said what is traumatic to you is your trauma, it is not someone else's. There is no judgment here on the "traumatic-ness" of your experience.

Now this exercise has three parts. So take your time and don't rush through it.

For the first part, write out the entire memory. Be as detailed and complete as you can. Make sure to establish the basic facts such as your age, when this happened, who was involved, and the emotions you experienced. Write down your reactions, your thoughts, and your feelings. Include the small details, the visuals, the senses, and the environment.

If you are having difficulty beginning this exercise then start writing about what was happening right before the incident. Then gradually work your way in.

If you're writing about a period in your life with multiple traumatic incidents then start with whichever one presents itself as the strongest. If you are having trouble piecing it together then maybe write out the timeline as a template to work from.

There are no set rules on writing about trauma. If you become overwhelmed, stop writing and return to it later. If you feel the need to just get it done, then go full stream of consciousness, don't worry about grammar or spelling, just get the damn words down on paper.

When you've got this first part completed as thoroughly as you can then it's time to take it even further into part two and write about how it has affected you and your life. Such as, how this has affected how you trust people, or your relationships, or your self-esteem. Also write about what it's like when something triggers this memory. Why you avoid certain situations and people because of this experience. The main objective here is to create the most vividly complete picture that you can, from past to present.

And now finally, with part three, condense the memory down into one succinct final sentence that states exactly what the memory is and what happened. But write it without the emotions. As if you are an impartial observer.

Some examples would be: *I was a child, I trusted the adult.* Or, *I was deep in my addiction at the time and I couldn't take care of myself, let alone anyone else.* Or, *I didn't do anything wrong, I was in the wrong place at the wrong time.*

Be objective. Be detached. Because this final part is where you are going to find acceptance. You are not making excuses. You are not letting anyone off the hook. You're accepting the reality of what really happened and letting go of whatever story you've been telling yourself.

* * *

When you're done put it away. You never have to read this piece again (if you don't want to). Leave that shit in the past. The trauma is over. By writing about it you have taken its power away and made it yours. Consider this exercise the final time you have to ever experience this memory again.

Now it's time to move on.

Take a moment and sit quietly. Think about your life as it is now. Think about how everything that you have experienced, good and bad, has brought you to this moment and shaped you into the person you are now. I know that all may sound cheesy. But here's the kicker.

Your past doesn't determine your future.

You do.

Putting It All Together

James Brown

If you're reading this, I'm assuming that you've made it through the whole book. Or at least I'm hoping you did. And I'm hoping, too, that you've done most if not all the exercises. If you have, you've completed the equivalent of two or three university-level classes in creative writing. Though our thematic focus has been on recovery, the exercises themselves involve the techniques and elements of storytelling. Character. Conflict. Dialogue. Scene. Setting and place. This is the stuff that goes into the making of a good story.

Now it's time to put together all the things you've learned from the exercises and write a complete short story. I'd say, just off the top of my head, that you're looking at anywhere from between 10 and 20 pages, possibly more, likely not less. Some of you might even feel inspired to embark on a novel or full-length memoir, and that's terrific, go for it, but maybe just not yet. Better to begin with baby-steps, and further hone your skills by first trying your hand at a short story, be it real or made-up, fiction or non-fiction, or a mixture of both.

Typically writers draw on their personal experience for material, and I highly recommend doing it, as it lends authenticity to your work. It's one real detail followed by another that makes for a good story regardless of whether the definition of "real" or "true" means altering the material facts to protect your identity or someone else's.

We've all seen movies that say they're "based on a true story," and I don't know what it is about that claim, but when we're told that it's a true story or close to it, it suddenly takes on greater emotional weight. The best stories, for me anyway, come from the heart, inspired by experience even if that experience is disguised.

Anne Lamott wrote a really good book about writing called *Bird by Bird*, and in it she credits the writer Alice Adams with coming up with a formula for a short story. I get worried when I hear about formulas for stories. I don't believe in them. The world is a complicated, messy place, and if good art is about trying to make sense out of that messiness and how it affects our equally messy lives, it's not a one-size-fits-all kind of thing. Formulas invariably result in bad writing with one-dimensional characters, cliches and predictable plots.

That said, however, Alice Adams is still onto something with her ABDCE structure for a short story, and, interestingly, some of the best stories I've read seem to break down along similar lines, or variations thereof. But let's stick to the basics for now.

A is for *Action*.
B is for *Background*.
D is for *Development*.
C is for *Climax*.
E is for *Ending*.

Action suggests starting your story with a scene. And in that scene there needs to be conflict. Without it, there's no story. Who wants to read about a perfectly happy person with a perfectly happy life free of worry, danger or trouble? I don't. That person has no reason to change, and I want to learn from other's troubles, how they fight to turn things around, and if, in the end, something important comes of their struggles. A simple but significant realization will do. The conflict can be anything you want, and as an alcoholic-addict you shouldn't have any problem coming up with an opening scene with conflict.

Think relationships.

Think environment.

Think about our own crazy minds spinning out of control. An entire story, by the way, can take place inside the head of a character. An excellent example of this is "The Yellow Wallpaper" by Charlotte Perkins Gilman where everything is filtered through the narrator's consciousness, and because the narrator goes insane over the course of the story, her perception of reality, like that of the alcoholic-addict, is a far cry from the others in her life.

Background is where you pull back and breathe some life into the character or characters you showed us in the opening scene. This is where we get to know them better, how they think and feel, maybe how they look and dress, where they are in time and place, and what happened to them in the past to make them the way they are today.

If you started strong in the opening with action and conflict, then you've got the reader's attention and can safely cruise for a page or two, building on the details of character that make them three-dimensional. The more we know about them, the more we understand them, the more apt we are to care about them. And we need to care, even if we don't necessarily like them. If they're portrayed as real people who share similar feelings, emotions and thoughts that we do, whether we agree or not with their life decisions, it's pretty hard to write them off as unworthy of our concern. Again, we don't have to like them, we just have to care.

Development is about returning to the conflict that you introduced in the beginning and building on it. This part of the formula has much to do with plot, how the story hereafter evolves and expands. It deals with the effects of the conflict and requires that your main character take action. But there are obstacles in their way. The conflict isn't easily resolved, and so the story is about the character's struggles, what they must confront and overcome to achieve their goal, like getting sober before you lose your family. Whatever the conflict, it presents a critical challenge that your character needs to tackle head-on or pay a heavy price for failing to do so, which leads us to the next part of the formula.

Climax (no, not that kind) is the peak of the story where the conflict collides with its opposition. It's a show-down of sorts, like that old shoot-out at the OK Corral, or like an alcoholic-addict coming home one morning, still wasted from the wild night before, and finding the living room packed with family and friends. The dreaded intervention.

At this point the story might erupt in a final struggle. In the OK Corral, the outlaws go down in a hail of gunfire with the Town Marshal and Special Police prevailing. In the intervention scenario, the climax could be the alcoholic-addict finally admitting that they have a problem and then being whisked off to rehab. The outcome of the climax doesn't necessarily resolve the initial conflict, but it sets the stage for its possibility.

That's for the last part.

Ending is about what happens *after* the climax. Hopefully there's been some growth for the character, especially for people like us in that intervention scenario. Hopefully there's been some serious reflection and self-evaluation resulting in a change for the better. This is where the very real possibility of growth and resolution occurs. At the same time this doesn't mean that your story has to end happily with all the loose ends tied neatly together. Life, as I said before, is a messy affair, and there's no rule saying that you can't end sadly, darkly, as so many of our stories do in real life. But I caution against it, and I'll explain why in a minute.

PUTTING IT ALL TOGETHER

First let me give you a quick example of a story I wrote, a real one, that meets most of the criteria of the ABDCE formula even though I didn't plan it that way. It's about a part of my life that I wished never happened, but it did, and it doesn't have a "happily ever after" ending.

I had a breakdown after the death of my ex-wife and started drinking again. The idea of killing myself seemed like a good one and that's where I begin the story. The opening scene, the *Action*, is about my meltdown at the kitchen table and going to the bedroom closet for my shotgun when my wife and one of my boys stop me. They corral me into the car. Their plan is to take me to a mental hospital but on the way there I jump out of the moving car, as does my twelve-year old boy, and together we make our way through the badlands of San Bernardino to a Hilton Hotel in the dead of the night.

I get us a room, order hot wings for my boy, and drinks for myself. It's here where I work in some *Background* material involving the events and personal history that led up to this insane night.

The next morning I call my wife, tell her where I am, and she sends a dear friend of mine over to pick up my son and me. The *Climax* occurs when I get home, and there they are, more friends and family.

It's an intervention. And I'm soon on my way to rehab.

I cover my time in recovery and the struggle to get sober, which is the *Development* part, and when the day arrives to leave rehab, the *End* of the story comes with a moment of realization as my wife is driving me home. It's a hopeful though guarded realization, and I write it in the third-person as if I'm seeing myself from a distance. In the car window, "he will glimpse the reflection of a hopeful man firmly determined to stay sober. In it, he will also glimpse what is burrowed deep inside his other self, the alcoholic, the addict, always waiting to reemerge."

The fact is that, yes, I've changed, I've learned from my own story, and yet there are no guarantees that I won't return to my self-destructive ways.

Above all, however, there is *hope*, and I can't stress this enough.

Hope is the single most important message I could possibly impart to myself, and, by extension, others on the comeback trail of addiction. Some of us are certain to give up and give in to the obsession to drink and use and we know how that ends. Death. Alienation. Institutions or prison. There aren't many of us who haven't lost a friend, lover or family member to an overdose or suicide. I'm not implying that there isn't value to the addiction story that ends darkly, predictably, because if nothing else it reinforces what we already know to be true.

On the other hand, if stories are about struggle, as I believe they are, and that struggle proves fruitless rather than transformative, then you have to ask yourself two basic questions.

Why did I take this journey? And what did I take away from it?

I really liked *Leaving Las Vegas* by John O'Brien, both novel and movie, and in them the main character sets out to literally drink himself to death. And he accomplishes it in a grand, repulsive finale. The author himself was an alcoholic, only he took a shortcut and shot himself before his movie came out. According to his father, that novel was his suicide note.

But what does his story mean, in so far as a story *means*? That a drunk who quits caring and completely gives us hope will die? It's like watching *Titanic* and knowing from the start how it's going to end.

I suppose that's fine. For some.

But it's not for me. Mr. O'Brien was a fine writer, and I would've liked to have seen what more he could've written if he'd gotten sober.

I also would've liked to have seen what my alcoholic brother, a young and accomplished actor who shot and killed himself, could've done with his career if he'd cleaned up. The same goes for my alcoholic sister, also an actor, who leaped to her death. On second thought, forget about their careers. I'd love nothing more than for us to just sit around in my sister's backyard on a lazy summer afternoon and have a barbeque and talk and smile and laugh again. As for myself, I certainly wouldn't be writing this if I'd finished what I started that night I lost all hope.

A good story doesn't sermonize. It doesn't preach. Leave that for the priests and pastors and gurus. The power of storytelling is in its ability to help others see themselves in ways that might not have otherwise been able to see through the dramatic portrayal of the human struggle. That's what I want from you. The truth minus the sermon.

So now we've gone full circle, returning us to the opening lines of what this book is about.

PUTTING IT ALL TOGETHER

It's about looking at yourself. It's about looking inside yourself and better understanding who you are, what makes you tick, and why.

That understanding empowers us to reverse the course of our self-destruction and concentrate on our recovery. You already know the story of the misery and anguish of addiction. You've lived it. You've written about it in the different exercises in this book and now that journey culminates in the writing of a full-length short story.

Maybe some of the pieces you wrote will find a place in your story.

Maybe one of them becomes your opening scene?

Or your last?

However you end up writing it, Patrick and I don't mind returning to hell with you. We resided there for decades. Both of us should've been dead many times over, and, in a way, as alcoholic-addicts, we *were* dead. When you take us deep into your personal hell, please consider making our stories of change and redemption a part of your own.

In embracing the lives of others like us, we embrace the tattered remains of our own past, and it's together, not alone, that we tell our stories with the hope of saving a life, one that belongs to us all.

So What Do We Do with This Book Now?

James Brown

What I like and fear most is sharing my story. It could be at an A.A. meeting. It could be in a recovery group. Doesn't matter. Opening yourself up to a bunch of relative strangers can be scary and intimidating. Soon as I start talking, I worry about what others might think of me.

I worry that I'll reveal too much about myself.

That people will think I'm sick or twisted or debased beyond redemption.

Most of all, I worry that they won't like me, and I want to be liked. I want to be accepted for who

I am *now*, or at least the person I'm struggling to become, and not the one I was when I was drinking and using and running amok. Fact is, if you've lived the life of an alcoholic-addict, there's not much you could've done that other drunks and junkies in the room haven't also done in some form or fashion, if not the exact same thing.

Our fears are unfounded.

We're more alike than different, and it's our similarities, as well as our differences that makes sharing our stories so instrumental to our recovery, sense of belonging, and peace of mind. And that's the part I like most about this time-honored practice.

I see myself in other's stories.

They likely see themselves in mine. It's consoling and comforting knowing that our personal experiences affirm commonalities and that I'm far from the only troubled soul in the room. Hearing the newcomer struggling to get sober reminds me of my own early struggles, which is a lesson I can't afford to forget. Hearing the person with years of sobriety shows me that getting and staying sober is more than a mere possibility but rather a lasting, wonderfully renewed way of life. If she can do it, I can do it.

Many years ago, when I walked into my first A.A. meeting, I was stunned by the stories

I heard. I couldn't believe that anyone in their right mind would be so open and honest about the insane things they did, the many people they hurt, how far they'd sunk and all they'd lost. Had they no shame? Weren't they embarrassed? I swore I'd never humiliate myself like them, but in time, as my addiction worsened and it became imperative that I change or die, I came to understand the importance of their openness and honesty with each other. The alcoholic-addict has to face the demons of their past and present head-on in order to defeat them, and we can't do that if we're so scared of being judged that we don't tell the truth, the whole truth and nothing but the truth in sharing our stories.

Which brings us to the question asked in the title of this chapter.

So What Do We Do with This Book Now?

Meaning what do we do with all these exercises Patrick and I have asked you to write.

The options vary depending on your situation. It could be that you stumbled across this book on your own and wanted to see if it could help you. It could also be that you wanted to learn a few things about creative writing in the process.

That's great.

This is exactly the sort of initiative and drive that goes into turning your life around as well as taking what might be your first step toward becoming a writer. In doing the assignments by yourself, for yourself, it's Patrick's and my sincere hope that our book will have a positive impact on your recovery. If it does, that means your hard work was worth every bit of the blood, sweat and tears you poured into it. And there's no law that says you have to show your writing to anyone. You've learned and grown from the act of writing itself and that's what matters most.

On the other hand, maybe you belong to a recovery writer's workshop and want to use a few of the assignments for your group. Or maybe you want to organize your own recovery writer's workshop and think this book would be a good place to start. Or maybe you're in rehab and your counselor wants to try it out in group. In these situations, we'd do with the exercises what we do with our spoken stories. Share them. But here's where it can get tricky.

It's one thing to talk in A.A. or in group. You've done that. You've likely even overcome much of your initial fear of sharing. But your personal writing? Passing copies of that around for everyone to read is a different beast. You might not be so comfortable with this idea, and I don't blame you.

I'm sure many of you put your heart and soul into your writing. Maybe you thought long and hard over what words to use and how best to arrange them into a sentence. Maybe you couldn't sleep at night because you were fretting about your characters, mulling over what they might say or do in a certain situation, and the next thing you know you had all these different voices in your head, chattering away. Rest assured, that's all part of the creative process, and it's enough to drive you crazy.

Writers, like their alcoholic-addict counterparts, are notoriously angst-ridden people. For good reason, too. They live inside their heads. They spend long hours alone in a room, trying to create something — a story, a novel, a poem — and if you've slaved over your writing and really care about it, letting others read and comment on it can be nerve-racking. Sharing your writing, like sharing in a meeting, requires courage.

So comes the dreaded day when you have to show your work to the world. That world, in one case, may be as small as one close friend. In another, it may be your peers in recovery, and the person overseeing the activity I'm about to describe is either your drug and alcohol counselor or the leader of your own writer's workshop.

When I teach creative writing, each student has to make copies of their own work and distribute it to the class one session in advance of their workshop date. This gives everyone a day or two to get your stuff read and prepare a written critique, which they share when we discuss your story. Other times, if we're not up against the clock, we skip the written critique and read the work in class.

So it goes like this:

1) You write the assignment. Hopefully you have access to a laptop and printer, so you can type and print it out, which makes it easier to read. I don't know about you, but my handwriting is practically illegible, even to me.

2) If you're in-patient, you can't just jump in a car, go to a copy center and make copies of your work (stopping off at the dope man's place on the way, so you can relapse and screw up your life again), so a staff member has to handle the copying part.

3) Everyone gets a copy of your work. Your counselor or workshop leader gives the group ten or fifteen minutes to read it, longer if it's a full story.

4) Then the discussion begins. And you, the author, can't join in right away. Why? So you don't put a damper on the open exchange of ideas, so you don't get caught up trying to defend yourself if you

feel you've been misinterpreted. Just chill and listen. You can answer questions and address your concerns after everyone has had their say.

In college we sit in a circle, like you do in group, and I go around the room and ask each student to *briefly* comment on the story or exercise. I stress *briefly*, a minute or two at most, so that no one person dominates the more reserved or shy ones in class. There will be plenty of time to talk when the instructor opens things up for discussion. And typically, so I don't unduly influence the students' opinions, I reserve my comments for the end.

The exception to my holding back until everyone has had a chance to share is when somebody oversteps their boundaries by being overly critical, negative, or downright rude. In my classes, there's no place for that kind of behavior, and I believe the same should hold true for recovery programs as well as recovery writer's workshops. Harsh or nonconstructive criticism doesn't help anyone, and it's the instructor's job to keep the order and protect the author from insult and injury.

I also suggest, for the recovery writer's workshop, that the leadership role rotate from one meeting to another, so that no one person "owns" the group. That can result in resentment and ego issues. Absolute power, as the saying goes, corrupts absolutely. Besides, if you have a shitty leader always running the show, it won't be long before your workshop falls apart and disbands.

The major difference between the approach to a university writer's workshop and that of a recovery program or recovery writer's workshop is that instead of focusing on creative writing techniques, the leader should guide the group to examine the exercises from the point-of-view of the alcoholic-addict and the recovery-related issues each gives rise to.

This isn't to say that in a recovery writer's workshop you *can't* address matters of creative writing technique, because I imagine some in the group might aspire to be writers independent of their addiction and would appreciate input along those lines. Nevertheless, I can't stress enough the risk of losing sight of our common and most important goal of sobriety. The emphasis should be on what brings us together, meaning that the discussion predominately focus on how a particular piece speaks to us as alcoholic-addicts.

In what ways do we see ourselves in it?

Do we identify?

How do we connect with it emotionally? Psychologically?

As alcoholic-addicts, our objective is to learn from the shared experiences of our creative expression.

In, for instance, the exercises dealing with God with a capital *G* and god with a lower-case *g*, use the issues the writer raises to generate a conversation on the importance of spirituality in recovery. On the exercises on relapse, use the writer's work as a bouncing board for members of the group to share their own feelings and stories on the subject.

What do you think sparked your own relapse, if you've had one?

How did you justify it? Rationalize it?

We can all come up with excuses, but is there such a thing as a good one for getting wasted again? I'm not so sure there is, but maybe I'm wrong. This would be a great time to open it up for discussion. And how about Patrick's exercise on lying, distorting the truth to conceal our real motives? Who among us hasn't told a small lie and watched it morph into a huge one that comes back to haunt us?

That should get the group talking.

Every exercise in this book is designed to generate an open and honest dialogue on the hardcore, real life issues that affect alcoholic-addicts on a daily basis. Through writing, as we move through our journey toward recovery, our once seemingly mortal wounds can begin to heal. With each new sentence, with each new scene or story we write, we discover ourselves in ways we never before thought possible. We gain distance on our lives and our addiction. We create a space between us and the written word. And in that space we find a greater sense of clarity about who we were, who we are now, and who we can become if we're willing to change, learn and grow.

Patrick and I want you to be creative.

We want you to embrace your artistic side and have some fun while you're at it. Recovery is about that light at the end of the tunnel, not darkness and gloom. So let yourself go. Invent. Dream. The power of the imagination is immeasurable, so use it to imagine a new and meaningful life for yourself and make it a reality.

About the Authors

JAMES BROWN is the author of the addiction memoirs, *Apology to the Young Addict*, *The Los Angeles Diaries*, and *This River*. He has received the Nelson Algren Award for Short Fiction and a National Endowment for the Arts Literature Fellowship. His writing has been featured in numerous publications, including *The New York Times Magazine*, *GQ*, *New England Review*, and *Ploughshares*. Brown is a Professor of English and Creative Writing at California State University, San Bernardino.

PATRICK O'NEIL is the author of the addiction memoir, *Gun, Needle, Spoon*. He holds an MFA in Creative Writing from Antioch University Los Angeles where he is an adjunct faculty member for their Continuing Education program. He is a practicing Certified Drug and Alcohol Counselor and is on the Board of Directors for REDEEMED, a non-profit Criminal Record Clearing Project that brings lawyers & professional writers together to help others move beyond their past. In 2016, for his exemplary work in the recovery community, O'Neil received a Governor's Pardon by California Governor Jerry Brown.

www.ingramcontent.com/pod-product-compliance
Lightning Source LLC
Chambersburg PA
CBHW020908080526
44589CB00011B/501